REXX in the TSO Environment

Books and Training Products From QED

DATABASE

Data Analysis: The Key to Data Base Design
The Data Dictionary: Concepts and Uses
DB2: The Complete Guide to Implementation and Use
Logical Data Base Design
DB2 Design Review Guidelines
DB2: Maximizing Performance of Online Production Systems
Entity-Relationship Approach to Logical Data Base Design
How to Use ORACLE SQL*PLUS
ORACLE: Building High Performance Online Systems
Embedded SQL for DB2: Application Design and Programming
SQL for dBASE IV
Introduction to Data and Activity Analysis
ORACLE Design Review Guidelines
Using DB2 to Build Decision Support Systems
How to Use SQL for DB2

SYSTEMS ENGINEERING

Handbook of Screen Format Design
Managing Projects: Selecting and Using PC-Based Project Management Systems
The Complete Guide to Software Testing
A User's Guide for Defining Software Requirements
A Structured Approach to Systems Testing
Practical Applications of Expert Systems
Expert Systems Development: Building PC-Based Applications
Storyboard Prototyping: A New Approach to User Requirements Analysis
The Software Factory: Managing Software Development and Maintenance
Data Architecture: The Information Paradigm
Advanced Topics in Information Engineering

MANAGEMENT

CASE: The Potential and the Pitfalls
Strategic and Operational Planning for Information Services
The State of the Art in Decision Support Systems
The Management Handbook for Information Center and End-User Computing
Disaster Recovery: Contingency Planning and Program Analysis

MANAGEMENT (cont'd)

Winning the Change Game
Information Systems Planning for Competitive Advantage
Critical Issues in Information Processing Management and Technology
Developing the World Class Information Systems Organization
The Technical Instructor's Handbook: From Techie to Teacher
Collision: Theory vs. Reality in Expert System
How to Automate Your Computer Center: Achieving Unattended Operations
Ethical Conflicts in Information and Computer Science, Technology, and Business

DATA COMMUNICATIONS

Data Communications: Concepts and Solutions
Designing and Implementing Ethernet Networks
Network Concepts and Architectures
Open Systems: The Guide to OSI and its Implementation
VAX/VMS: Mastering DCL Commands and Utilities

PROGRAMMING

VSAM Techniques: Systems Concepts and Programming Procedures
How to Use CICS to Create On-Line Applications: Methods and Solutions
DOS/VSE/SP Guide for Systems Programming: Concepts, Programs, Macros, Subroutines
Systems Programmer's Problem Solver
VSAM: Guide to Optimization and Design
MVS/TSO: Mastering CLISTS
MVS/TSO: Mastering Native Mode and ISPF
VAX/VMS: Mastering DCL Commands and Utilities

SELF-PACED TRAINING

SQL as a Second Language
Building Online Production Systems with DB2 (Video)
Introduction to UNIX (CBT)
Building Production Applications with ORACLE (Video)

For Additional Information or a Free Catalog contact

QED INFORMATION SCIENCES, INC. • P. O. Box 82-181 • Wellesley, MA 02181
Telephone: 800-343-4848 or 617-237-5656

REXX in the TSO Environment

Gabriel F. Gargiulo

QED Information Sciences, Inc.
Wellesley, Massachusetts

© 1990 by QED Information Sciences, Inc.
P.O. Box 82-181
Wellesley, MA 02181

Library of Congress Number: 90-8506
International Standard Book Number: 0-89435-354-3

Printed in the United States of America
90 91 92 10 9 8 7 6 5 4 3 2 1

Library of Congress Cataloging-in-Publication Data

Gargiulo, Gabriel F.
    REXX in the TSO environment / Gabriel F. Gargiulo.
        p. cm.
    Includes index.
    ISBN 0-89435-354-3
    1. REXX (Computer program language) 2. Time-sharing computer systems.
I Title.
    QA76.73.R24G37   1990
    005.2'25--dc20

To my sons,
Marc and Michael

CONTENTS

PREFACE

REXX is the most exciting language you'll find on IBM's mainframe systems. REXX is modern, different, and robust. IBM has positioned REXX to serve as a common development language on its MVS, VM, and PS2 operating systems. Learning REXX opens the door to mastery of TSO and CMS, and makes using DB2 and SQL/DS much easier.

I have long derived pleasure from the study and use of spoken languages, and with the coming of REXX, from computer languages as well. I hope this book makes it easy for you to pick up "native fluency" in REXX.

Your suggestions and comments are welcome, and should be addressed to me in care of QED.

I created this book from start to finish using WordPerfect 5.0, a Toshiba T1200 portable computer and a Hewlett Packard Laserjet IIP printer. I have learned much about desktop publishing by writing this book, and can thank Beth Roberts and Edwin Kerr of QED for their patience and support throughout the process.

Join me in exploring this fascinating language on your TSO system.

Gabe Gargiulo

INTRODUCTION

Imagine learning a new modern language that is spoken in all major foreign countries, that enables you to travel without fear of being isolated! Imagine being sure that your efforts are not wasted, because everyone else is also learning that language! And what if that language were almost exactly like English so your task wasn't very difficult at all?

REXX is like that. REXX is IBM's answer to the tower of Babel that it created with MVS, VM, and the personal computer all speaking wildly different languages.

Now you can move about with ease, knowing that you will be understood. REXX is available on three of IBM's major operating systems, MVS, VM, and the Personal Computer.

You can be sure that what you learn will not go out of style, because IBM is heavily promoting REXX, as its Flagship user interface language, and is creating connections to it all throughout its landscape of program products. You can go into QMF (Query Management Facility, a subset of DB2 and SQL/DS database management systems), and find a connection to REXX, in the Forms Panel, under Calculations. You can go into JCL, and there find it's possible to execute a REXX program through JCL that eliminates the need for any further JCL. In Netview, a program product used by operations and support personnel, you'll find REXX ready and waiting for you.

This book is about the REXX language as it is found on IBM's MVS (Multiple Virtual Storage) operating system, in the program development system known as TSO (Time Sharing Option). It is a real world approach to REXX and does not pull any punches. You will learn REXX as is currently implemented under TSO. You will not learn a watered down version of REXX as it is implemented under some other operating system. You can immediately become more productive on TSO with this book, because you will learn how to put commonly done tasks into a short program, and run the program, instead of always typing in a series of commands.

With this book you can be more useful to your employer at once, because you will learn a language that communicates with TSO, the ISPF Dialogue Manager, the ISPF Editor, the program product Netview, DB2 (DataBase 2), and SQL (Structured Query Language), and the QMF (Query Management Facility) Forms panels. In addition you won't have to learn a new language to work with VM/CMS (Virtual Machine/Conversational Monitor System), because you'll find essentially the same REXX language there.

The emphasis will be on how things work, with a minimum of time spent on the theoretical aspects of the language. You will learn fast with this book, because you can try out the examples on your system, and practice with the computer problems on your system. In doing the computer problems you will build up a library of extremely useful and pertinent examples of all the aspects of the REXX language, that you and others will find invaluable when creating REXX programs.

This book assumes that you know something about TSO commands, such as ALLOCATE, and LISTDS. This is because the main reason why REXX exists is to pass TSO commands to TSO. This enables you to gain control over TSO. You can get this knowledge by using TSO commands for at least 6 months, or by doing the exercises in my book on TSO, "MVS/TSO: Mastering Native Mode and ISPF", QED March 1990.

If you aren't familiar with TSO commands you can still benefit from this book, because I generally tell you in the workshops what the TSO command you need looks like, and if that isn't enough, you can check Appendix A for the exact form of the TSO command you need.

In this book you'll learn how to do the following with REXX:
1. Pass commands to TSO and ISPF
2. Interact with the terminal
3. Manipulate strings of data
4. Create new functions and/or subroutines
5. Write programs that repeat, with REXX's loop control structure
6. Interact with TSO commands that ask for information
7. Intercept and use information displayed by TSO commands
8. Read and write records in disk files
9. Manipulate data using arrays of variables
10. Use TSO's internal data queue, known as the stack
11. Create ISPF EDIT macros

You will find a valuable reference for REXX functions in Appendix B, and one for REXX instructions in Appendix C. Appendix E contains a thought provoking proposal for phasing out JCL.

Who should read this book? This book is designed for programmers, end users, database administrators, production support personnel, operations personnel, support personnel, and anyone who needs more than just the basic system supplied by IBM. Anyone who wants or needs the ability to create programs for him/herself with a minimum of effort and overhead should read this book.

Structure of the Book

The book is presented in separate chapters, and five appendixes. Study each chapter, and do the workshops on the computer. In many workshops we show you the results you should expect. Appendix A contains the solutions to all the workshops. Save your answers to the workshops, and you'll own a complete library of every imaginable type of REXX program you'll ever need.

Chapter 1

WHAT YOU CAN DO WITH REXX

This chapter will show you some of the things you can do with REXX. You will get an idea of REXX's capabilities.

Topics:

1.1 Main Function of REXX
1.2 Automate Repetitive Tasks
1.3 Interact with the Dialogue Manager
1.4 Create New Commands
1.5 Personal Programming Tasks
1.6 Questions/Problems

1.1 MAIN FUNCTION OF REXX

REXX's main purpose is to pass commands to TSO, and/or the Dialogue Manager of TSO/ISPF (see Figure 1.1). Using REXX's built-in logic and control structures, you can make that a very easy and error free task. You can use REXX very effectively even if you don't ever pass a command to TSO or ISPF. REXX is a complete programming language in itself and doesn't need a TSO or an ISPF for it to be useful. Before we go any further, I want to emphasise that you can do practically anything with REXX, and that the limits

1

should be only that which you haven't thought of yet, not any inherent limits of the programming system. If it can be done, do it, and use REXX!

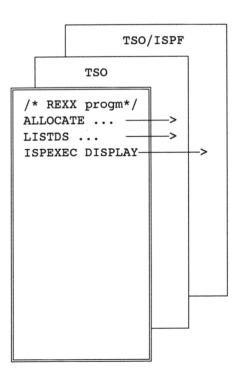

Figure 1.1. Passing commands to TSO, and/or TSO/ISPF.

1.2 AUTOMATE REPETITIVE TASKS

Sometimes you find yourself keying in a series of commands over and over again (see Figure 1.2). These commands can be placed within a REXX program, (see Figure 1.3) and you can have REXX pass those commands to TSO, or TSO/ISPF. This eliminates any errors associated with keying things all over again. Take my advice, put the commands in a REXX program, execute the REXX program, and you'll be sure that the commands are right.

```
ALLOCATE DSN('SYSTEM.INPUT.DATA') SHR DDN(INFILE)

ALLOCATE DSN(*) DDN(REPORT)

CALL MYLIB.PROGRAMS(REPRTPGM)

SEND 'THE REPORT IS READY' U(TSOU02)
```

Figure 1.2. Commands you might execute frequently.

```
/* REXX SAMPLE */

"ALLOCATE DSN('SYSTEM.INPUT.DATA') SHR DDN(INFILE)"

"ALLOCATE DSN(*) DDN(REPORT)"

"CALL MYLIB.PROGRAMS(REPRTPGM)"

"SEND 'THE REPORT IS READY' U(TSOU02)"
```

Figure 1.3. Frequently executed commands placed in a REXX program.

1.3 INTERACT WITH THE DIALOGUE MANAGER

The TSO/ISPF Dialogue Manager provides you with the ability to create and display custom made panels, (See Figure 1.4) and to store and retrieve variables in the same or different sessions. You can create sets of panels and/or menus, much like ISPF itself.

```
┌─────────────────────────────────────────────┐
│                                             │
│        CUSTOM DATA ENTRY PANEL              │
│                                             │
│                                             │
│        NAME    _____             │
│                                             │
│        ADDRESS _____               │
│                                             │
│        TELEPHONE _____               │
│                                             │
│                                             │
│                                             │
│        PRESS ENTER TO ACCEPT                │
│                                             │
│        PF3 TO CANCEL                        │
│                                             │
└─────────────────────────────────────────────┘
```

Figure 1.4. Possible customized panel you can create with ISPF dialogue manager.

1.4 CREATE NEW COMMANDS

With REXX you can create programs that behave as if they were new TSO commands. For example, there is a TSO command TIME, that tells you the current time. You might create a REXX program named DATE, that tells you the current date. This new program can be executed just like the TSO command TIME, that is, you just type in its name, "DATE", and you are shown the current date. (See Figure 1.5) You might want to create new commands that work together with existing TSO commands, to provide an added measure of protection (see Figure 1.6). These new commands, as well as the old ones, can all be executed while you are in Line Mode TSO, sometimes called "Ready Mode", or "Native TSO", or while you are in ISPF, from practically any entry panel (see Figure 1.7). Notice that you must preface your command with "TSO", so ISPF will know you are talking to TSO, not to ISPF.

```
READY

TIME

11:22:03 03:08:90 CPU TIME 4.3 SVC UNITS 55433

DATE

TODAY IS THURSDAY MARCH 8 1990, HAPPY BIRTHDAY SUE!
```

Figure 1.5. Within "Ready Mode TSO". Executing the TSO command TIME, then the possible new command DATE, written as a REXX program.

```
===> ERASE PROGRAM1.COBOL

     ARE YOU SURE? REPLY Y/N

     Y

     PROGRAM1.COBOL     ERASED

     READY
```

Figure 1.6. Example of protecting against inadvertent erasure, using a REXX program.

```
                        ISPF-MVS PRIMARY OPTION MENU
SELECT OPTION ===> TSO DATE

  0  ISPF PARMS  - SPECIFY TERMINAL AND SPF PARAMETERS TIME 11:0
  1  BROWSE      - DISPLAY SOURCE DATA OR OUTPUT LIST TERMINAL7
  2  EDIT        - CREATE OR CHANGE SOURCE DATA          PF KEYS-12
  3  UTILITIES   - PERFORM SPF UTILITY FUNCTIONS
  4  FOREGROUND  - COMPILE, ASSEMBLE, LINK EDIT, OR DEBUG
  5  BACKGROUND  - COMPILE, ASSEMBLE, OR LINK EDIT
  6  COMMAND     - ENTER TSO COMMAND OR CLIST
  7  SUPPORT     - TEST DIALOG OR CONVERT MENU/MESSAGE
  T  TUTORIAL    - DISPLAY INFORMATION ABOUT SPF
  X  EXIT        - TERMINATE SPF USING LIST/LOG DEFAULTS

  PRESS END KEY TO TERMINATE SPF
```

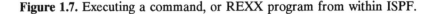

Figure 1.7. Executing a command, or REXX program from within ISPF.

1.5 PERSONAL PROGRAMMING TASKS

REXX is so easy to use that you may want to use it for those short (or long) programs that help you out in your everyday affairs. For example, you might frequently be calculating disk space to be used by your files. Instead of doing this with a calculator, you could create a REXX exec to do it (see Figure 1.8).

```
    ==> %spacecal

    PLEASE ENTER RECORD LENGTH 80

    PLEASE ENTER BLOCK SIZE     8000

    PLEASE ENTER NUMBER OF RECORDS 10000

    YOU   NEED 500 CYLINDERS
```

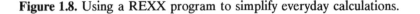

Figure 1.8. Using a REXX program to simplify everyday calculations.

1.6 QUESTIONS/PROBLEMS

Q 1.1: Can REXX be used to protect the user from his/her errors?

Q 1.2: List three TSO commands that are potentially destructive and could benefit from some protection using REXX.

Chapter 2

REXX ON TSO

This chapter is about the very practical aspects of REXX programs as they are found in the TSO environment. I'll tell you the difference between a REXX program and a CLIST, and how TSO knows the difference. Finally, I'll point out how a REXX Exec and a CLIST are executed and how they are similar in this respect.

Topics:

2.1 What is a REXX Program?
2.2 Differences between CLIST and REXX
2.3 How does TSO know which one?
2.4 Differences in Allocation
2.5 Differences/Similarities in Execution
2.6 Questions/Problems

2.1 WHAT IS A REXX PROGRAM?

A REXX program is a file, or dataset that has been cataloged, and whose name ends in EXEC. It is a disk file, since TSO can only, for all practical purposes, access disk files. The file contains records. Each record contains one or more TSO commands, and/or REXX instructions. In Figure 2.1, the dataset REXXPGMS.EXEC is a REXX program. You cannot tell from the name alone whether it is a library or not.

A REXX program is executed interactively at the terminal. That is, you execute it, and wait while it executes. You can control it while it executes, in other words, you can cancel it, and stop its execution. Generally you cannot do anything else while it executes, because it ties up your terminal.

Most users of TSO will place their REXX programs into libraries, also known as PDS's (Partitioned Data Sets), which may contain one or more other programs.

9

If written in a certain way, which we will demonstrate in the appropriate chapter, your REXX program may be used as a subcommand of the ISPF editor. Then it will be known as an Edit macro. If you know CLISTs, you will have realized that all we have said about REXX programs so far, is similar to CLISTs. The differences are in allocation, execution, and the contents, or the actual language used.

```
===> LISTCAT

REXXPGMS.EXEC
OLDPGMS.CLIST
PROGRAM1.COBOL
PROGRAM2.CNTL
```

Figure 2.1. List of possible datasets owned by a user.

2.2 DIFFERENCES BETWEEN CLIST AND REXX

Most people who have used TSO for any length of time have used CLISTs. (See Figure 2.2) CLIST language can do practically anything that REXX can, but the language itself is inferior. CLIST stands for Command LIST. For a time it was all there was on TSO, and so, if you wanted to write interactive programs on TSO you had to use CLISTs. There was no way of designating a literal, and no consistent way of indicating that something was a variable. Worse yet, the ampersand (&) was used in a capricious manner in conjunction with variables. Sometimes you used it, sometimes you didn't. In order to manipulate strings of characters, it was often necessary to nest the &STR and &SUBSTR functions, leading to very obscure coding. One could tolerate the mathematical insufficiencies of CLIST language, but found it difficult to manage with the inadequate control structures. With all due credit, IBM added some good control structures to CLIST language in recent times, such as a controlled DO loop, and a subroutine call. The worst thing about CLIST language was that CLISTs existed nowhere else in the world, and were like nothing else. If you learned CLISTs, you couldn't take that knowledge anywhere.

One point to remember: If a CLIST expects three positional parameters when it is executed, TSO will ask you for them one at a time. This is not true of REXX. If you don't supply the positional parameters, TSO will not ask you for them.

CLIST	REXX
old	new
bad for data strings	good string handling
lots of &&&&&	English-like
obscure at times	clear
good control structures	excellent control structures
bad for math	good for math
unique	common
prompts for positional parms	no prompting for positional parms

Figure 2.2 Differences between CLIST and REXX.

2.3 HOW DOES TSO KNOW WHICH ONE?

Since CLIST and REXX are two separate languages, TSO must have a way of knowing which language it is looking at. Anytime there can be ambiguity you must start off your REXX program with a comment containing the word "REXX" (Figure 2.3). I recommend that you always start your REXX program with the comment and the word "REXX". Do this until IBM declares that CLIST is officially dead, and that all CLISTs must be thrown into the shredder.

```
CLIST

PROC 1 DSET
/* MY CLIST PROGRAM*/
ALLOCATE DSNAME(&DSET)



REXX

/*REXX PROGRAM */ <----
ARG DSET
"ALLOCATE DSNAME("DSET")"
```

Figure 2.3. Required comment at beginning of REXX exec.

2.4 DIFFERENCES IN ALLOCATION

When you use a library to contain your REXX programs, you generally link (with the ALLOCATE command) the library to a symbolic file name, known in MVS as a DDNAME (Data Definition Name) (see Figure 2.4). This allows TSO to more easily access all the programs that are in the library. I recommend you do this: put REXX execs all in a library, and link the library to the symbolic file name SYSEXEC. Do not put any CLISTs in the same library. Doing this will let TSO search through your exec library before it searches through CLIST libraries. In addition, it will make it easier to convert over to exclusive use of REXX execs, when that time comes.

CLIST libraries still have to be allocated to the DDNAME SYSPROC. This hasn't changed. But you may place REXX execs in these libraries as well. I recommend you don't do this, but keep REXX and CLIST programs separate.

You may as well note right here, that your installation may not have installed TSO with the ability to search through libraries allocated to DDNAME SYSEXEC. If you put REXX execs in libraries allocated to DDNAME SYSEXEC, and TSO can't find them you need to execute this TSO command right after you log on: EXECUTIL SEARCHDD(YES) (See Figure 2.5).

```
ALLOC DDNAME(SYSEXEC) SHR DSN(MYREXX.EXEC)
```

Figure 2.4. Allocation of an Exec library to DDNAME SYSEXEC.

```
        READY

   ==> ALLOC DDNAME(SYSEXEC) SHR DSN(MYREXX.EXEC)
   ==> %MYEXEC
       COMMAND MYEXEC NOT FOUND
   ==> EXECUTIL SEARCHDD(YES)
   ==> %MYEXEC
       (COMMAND WORKS SUCCESSFULLY)
     ' READY
```

Figure 2.5. Commands and replies from TSO, showing failure because the installation had not installed TSO with SYSEXEC; and the command needed to activate SYSEXEC.
= = > shows commands typed in.

2.5 DIFFERENCES/SIMILARITIES IN EXECUTION

The way you execute your REXX exec depends on whether it is in a library or not, and whether the library has been allocated to one of the DDNAMEs SYSEXEC or SYSPROC. If your program is in a library, and that library has been allocated to the DDNAME SYSEXEC or SYSPROC, you may execute it the very simplest way possible: you just put a percent sign (%) in front of the program's member name in the library.   This is known as implicit execution (see Figure 2.6). Note this is exactly the same as the way it's done with CLISTs. If the above allocation has not been done, you'll have to execute the program the other way, known as explicit execution (see Figure 2.7).

%MYREXX

Figure 2.6. Implicit execution using percent sign.

EXEC REXXPGM.EXEC 'parameters' EXEC

Figure 2.7. Explicit execution using keyword EXEC.

2.6 QUESTIONS/PROBLEMS

Q 2.1: What language is this program written in?

```
/*REXX EXEC TO COMPILE MY PROGRAM*/
COBOL PROG1 SOURCE XREF
```

Q 2.2: What language is this program written in?

```
/*COMMAND PROCEDURE TO COMPILE MY PROGRAM*/
COBOL PROG1 SOURCE XREF
```

Q 2.3: If you allocate your REXX program library as follows, how must you execute it?

```
ALLOC DDN(SYSEXOC) SHR DSN(MYPROGS.EXEC)
```

Chapter 3

CHARACTERISTICS OF REXX

This chapter will show you what REXX is like as a language, and explain its major characteristics. It will compare REXX to several major programming languages in use today.

Topics:

3.1 What is REXX like?
3.2 Questions/Problems

3.1 WHAT IS REXX LIKE?

REXX is a programming language that was designed by Michael Cowlishaw, with the feedback of large numbers of IBM programmers. This makes it a unique language, with strong characteristics, unlike a language designed by a committee. It combines the best features of several programming languages, but slavishly imitates none. If you want something to compare REXX to, it has to be PLI, because REXX looks most like PLI. The resemblance is purely superficial, however. REXX is much simpler than PLI. Furthermore REXX does not have data typing, while PLI has strong data typing. In REXX all variables are numeric or character depending on what type of data they contain. There are no declarations that state what type of data a variable can contain.

It is a procedural language, so you must still perform each operation in the right sequence. REXX is a high-level language, and so is far removed from the native language of the CPU (Central Processing Unit, the part of a computer that executes instructions). You'll still have to put instructions in the right order to make things work.

REXX is a general purpose language, that is it is not intended mainly for mathematical programming, nor for business type programming.

REXX contains all the modern components of structured programming, namely the Sequence, the Conditional, the Case, and the Repetition. These components are implemented in a straightforward manner in REXX, so they don't have to be worked into your program in a roundabout manner. If you like programming, and have wished for a language that liked you, you'll like REXX.

REXX is essentially a free form language, with no restrictions as to columns. It uses very simple punctuation, and then only when needed to eliminate possible ambiguity. REXX is a long way from JCL (Job Control Language).

Perhaps the most significant feature of REXX is its full featured handling of data strings, known as Parsing, that is manipulating words within sentences, and character strings. This feature is often the hardest for Cobol programmers to adjust to. It is not like anything else, but it is appreciated by those needing to manipulate often unpredictable character strings.

REXX is mathematically complete, and will do arithmetic to any precision, in other words with any number of significant digits. REXX uses decimal numbers internally, so as to avoid conversion errors. You need not worry about accuracy of results.

In addition, to firmly place REXX in the present day, the author of REXX gave it the capability of approximating equality, rather than insisting on absolute down to the last decimal digit accuracy.

A characteristic that will appear after you have studied REXX for a while is that it has very few instructions. It doesn't need as many instructions as other languages, because REXX has a large number of built in functions, and allows you to very easily create functions of your own.

Another unique feature of REXX is its compound variables, similar to arrays or Cobol occurs clauses. You can do all manner of indexing and subscripting with these, and even use them to simulate a form of random access memory.

Interestingly enough, REXX does not have any type of file input or output of its own. Instead it depends on the operating system having that capability, and of communicating with REXX. Indeed, that is the way file input and output is realized under TSO and CMS. REXX uses EXECIO, which is actually a TSO command.

3.2 QUESTIONS/PROBLEMS

Q 3.1: What 2 significant language features does REXX lack?

Q 3.2: How is the lack of Input-Output made up for?

Chapter 4

EXAMPLE OF A REXX PROGRAM

This chapter will enable you to familiarize yourself with a simple REXX program, and will point out some of the major features of a REXX program.

Topics:

4.1 Sample Program
4.2 Questions/Problems

4.1 SAMPLE PROGRAM

```
1        /*SAMPLE REXX PROGRAM*/
2        A = 1
3        B = 2
4        C = A + B
5        SAY "THE ANSWER IS "    C
6        EXIT
```

Figure 4.1. Sample REXX program.

Take a look at the sample REXX program in Figure 4.1. This program doesn't do very much, but it will help us get started with REXX. The numbers that are in a vertical column to the left of the program are not

17

actually part of the program. When you examine your program using a text editor such as ISPF EDIT, you will see these numbers. When you run your REXX program, if you ever get a syntax error, REXX will refer to those same line numbers. We will use them here just for referencing the lines of the program. We won't use them again after that.

Let's start with line 1. This is a comment and tells us that this is a sample REXX program. It also tells TSO that it is a REXX program. You must start your REXX program under TSO with a comment like it. Specifically, line 1 must start with /*, and the word REXX must be in the comment. You must end the comment on the same line or on another line.

Line 2 is the simplest of REXX statements. It is an assignment statement. It puts a "1" into the variable "A".

Line 3 does something similar.

Line 4 asks REXX to place the sum of the variable "A" and the variable "B" into the variable "C".

Line 5 displays "THE ANSWER IS 3" on the terminal.

Line 6 ends the program. The word EXIT will always end your REXX program, and send control back to TSO, or ISPF, or wherever you were when you executed the program. You can, however, omit the word EXIT, if it would be the last statement on the last line. If there are no more instructions or statements in the program, that ends the program too.

I would like to point out, that if you desire, you can end the program with a *return code*. For example you might end the program with EXIT 10. That would end the program with the *return code* "10". All this does is to pass the number 10 to TSO or the program that called it. The program that called your program can examine the *return code* and take some action based on it, if it wishes. This is totally optional, and as a matter of fact, I wouldn't do it unless I were sure that my program were being called by another program that was going to examine *return code*.

4.2 QUESTIONS/PROBLEMS

Q 4.1: What must a REXX program always start with?

Q 4.2: What word, or instruction in REXX means to display upon the terminal?

Q 4.3: What does this program do?

```
/*REXX SAMPLE*/
X = 10
Y = 20
Z = Y - X
SAY "THE ANSWER IS " Z
```

Chapter 5

CHOOSING BETWEEN SEQUENTIAL AND PARTITIONED

In this chapter I'd like to point out the advantages and disadvantages of the the two types of datasets you can use to hold your Rexx programs, *sequential*, and *partitioned*.

I hope you'll opt for partitioned and use that for the workshops in the book, but if you don't, you'll still be able to do almost all the workshops in the book.

Topics:

5.1 Comparison of Sequential and Partitioned

5.1 COMPARISON OF SEQUENTIAL AND PARTITIONED

In Figure 5.1 you'll see a table that compares sequential and partitioned types of datasets. A sequential dataset is one that contains only one program. The entire file is your program, and nothing else. A partitioned dataset is a library that contains one or more programs.

Most programmers on TSO use partitioned, because they find it more convenient to place all their programs in one file. This makes it easier to keep track of all of one's programs. I hope you'll choose partitioned for your programs. If you do, you'll be able to create EDIT macros, and to execute your programs by just typing in their name, with or without a percent sign before them. The next two chapters will tell you more about executing your programs.

Partitioned also lets you create and use a whole library of custom built functions that parallel and supplement the functions that are built into REXX. I wish that partitioned made everything easier. Unfortunately it doesn't. The concatenation that you'll need to do with Partitioned is cumbersome. But you'll most likely need to do it only once. Even better, your installation might have set up an automatic concatenation that is done after you log on to TSO. If so, you won't mind using partitioned at all.

```
              Sequential

Good for one time program

Less convenient to execute

No DD Concatenation needed

Less efficient space use

Less common

Compress never needed
```

```
              Partitioned

Good for permanent programs

Convenient to execute

Concatenation recommended,
to SYSEXEC

Concatenation cumbersome

Good space utilization

More common

Compress needed periodically

Easy to execute, once
the concatenation done

Can build set of custom
functions

Can create EDIT macros
```

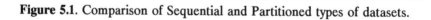

Figure 5.1. Comparison of Sequential and Partitioned types of datasets.

Chapter 6

HOW TO CREATE AND EXECUTE A SEQUENTIAL REXX EXEC

This chapter will show you step-by-step how you should create and execute a REXX program contained in a sequential dataset. If you have been creating and executing sequential CLISTs you should have no difficulty here, and may even skip this chapter if you wish.

If, on the other hand, you have never created a REXX program or a CLIST, you may want to follow the steps shown in this chapter from start to finish.

Topics:

6.1 Creating a Sequential Exec
6.2 Executing a Sequential Exec
6.3 Questions/Problems

6.1 CREATING A SEQUENTIAL EXEC

Follow these steps one after another, to create and execute a sequential REXX program. There may be other ways of doing this that are just as good, but if you follow these steps you're sure to wind up with a usable program.

I'm assuming you are using ISPF in your installation. ISPF has an excellent editor, and a panel for creating datasets. If you aren't already in ISPF, go into it now. Your installation manager can show you how, but generally you just type in "ISPF" after logging on to TSO.

Choose Option 3.2, from the ISPF Main Menu, or Primary Options Panel. (see Figure 6.1). You should now be looking at something like Figure 6.1. If you aren't, ask someone how to get to the Dataset Utility Allocate panel. There are two things to type in on this panel. "A" for Allocate in the SELECT OPTION field, and the name of your program in the field DATASET NAME. The only requirement here for a REXX program, is that

21

the name end in .EXEC. I have entered the name REXXPGM.EXEC on the panel in Figure 6.1. Now press ENTER. You should now see something like Figure 6.2. It is very likely that the attributes shown on your screen will not be the ones you see here. This is no problem. Just type over them, changing them to what you see here.

There are two items I can't help you with here, because they are installation dependant. They are Volume Serial and Generic Unit. Ask someone what to type in here. If you can't find someone, you can usually omit Volume Serial, and TSO will accommodatingly supply a Volume Serial number. As for Generic Unit, if your installation requires you to specify something here, you will have to find out what that is. If you guess, you may find yourself with a program on an illegal disk pack, and someone may delete it on you. Press ENTER. You should see the message "Dataset Allocated" in the upper right of your screen.

Now let's go into the dataset we have allocated and key in the lines of our program (See Figure 6.3). From the main menu, or primary option menu, choose option 2, the ISPF editor.

Figure 6.4 is the editor entry panel. It needs only one piece of information, the name of the dataset you allocated in previous steps. Key it in the field "DATASET NAME". Press ENTER. I hope this isn't your first time using the ISPF editor. If you haven't used it before, this is the time to look for my book on TSO and ISPF, "MVS/TSO: Mastering Native Mode and ISPF", QED March 1990. Press ENTER.

Now you're in the editor, and should be looking at a panel like the one in Figure 6.5, except that your program won't have been keyed in just yet. That's what you'll do now. Reminder: the comment goes first, and columns are not significant with REXX. I suggest one statement or instruction per line.

When you're satisfied that your program looks good, you can save it and execute it. Type SAVE on the command line, and press ENTER (see Figure 6.6).

6.2 EXECUTING YOUR SEQUENTIAL EXEC.

I'll show you how to execute your program while you're still in the editor as shown in Figure 6.7. This makes it easier for you to correct your program when the inevitable mishap occurs, because you will never leave the editor, and so will not have to go back into the editor.

Type in the command in the command line area, as shown. The command to execute your program is TSO EXEC program name EXEC. The TSO is required, since you are still in ISPF, and you need to prefix line mode TSO commands with "TSO" in order to execute them. The first EXEC tells TSO to look at this as a CLIST or REXX exec to be executed. Next you place your program name. You do not need the full name of your program, just the middle part, minus your userid, and minus the EXEC part of the name. Last, you specify EXEC once again. This is needed so TSO will know that you are executing a REXX program, not a CLIST. If your REXX program needs to have parameters passed to it at execution time, do it this way (see Figure 6.8). Place them all within one set of apostrophes. The apostrophes are not passed to your program. They are needed so TSO knows there are parameters.

It's possible that one of the parameters needs apostrophes around it (see Figure 6.9). This usually occurs with dataset names, since TSO requires apostrophes around dataset names that do not belong to you. If a parameter needs apostrophes, you have to double those apostrophes. This means two consecutive apostrophes, not the quotation mark. The double apostrophes are changed to single ones and passed to your program as single apostrophes. So the parameter ONE in this panel, would appear in your program as 'ONE'. Reminder: the apostrophe after REXXPGM and the one after TWO are there because this manner of executing programs requires apostrophes if there are parameters.

```
                           ┌──────────┐
                           │ ISPF 3.2 │
                           └──────────┘
---------------------------------DATASET UTILITY -------------------------
SELECT OPTION ===> A

   A - ALLOCATE NEW DATASET            C - CATALOG DATASET
   R - RENAME ENTIRE DATASET           U - UNCATALOG DATASET
   D - DELETE ENTIRE DATASET

   BLANK - DISPLAY DATASET INFORMATION

SPF LIBRARY
   PROJECT ===>
   LIBRARY ===>
   TYPE    ===>

OTHER PARTITIONED OR SEQUENTIAL DATASET
   DATASET NAME   ===> REXXPGM.EXEC
   VOLUME SERIAL ===>        (IF NOT CATALOGUED, REQUIRED FOR OPTION "C")
```

Figure 6.1. Allocating and creating a Sequential REXX program.

```
                      ┌───────────────────────────┐
                      │ Allocating with ISPF utility │
                      └───────────────────────────┘
---------------ALLOCATE NEW DATASET ---------------------------------
DATASET NAME 'TSOU01.REXXPGM.EXEC'

   VOLUME SERIAL      ===>        (BLANK FOR AUTHORIZED DEFAULT VOLUME)
   GENERIC UNIT       ===>
   SPACE UNITS        ===> TRKS   (BLKS, TRKS, OR CYLS)
   PRIMARY QUANTITY   ===> 1      (IN ABOVE UNITS)
   SECONDARY QUAN     ===> 1      (IN ABOVE UNITS)
   DIRECTORY BLOCKS   ===> 0      (ZERO FOR SEQUENTIAL DATASET)
   RECORD FORMAT      ===> VB
   RECORD LENGTH      ===> 255
   BLOCK SIZE         ===> 1680
```

Figure 6.2. The Attribute panel filled in.

```
                           ┌─────────────┐
                           │ Choose EDIT │
                           └─────────────┘
                              SPF-MVS PRIMARY OPTION MENU
     SELECT OPTION ===> 2
                           ─
     0   SPF PARMS     - SPECIFY TERMINAL AND SPF PARAMETERS   TIME 11:06
     1   BROWSE        - DISPLAY SOURCE DATA OR OUTPUT LISTINGS TERMINAL 3278
     2   EDIT          - CREATE OR CHANGE SOURCE DATA           PF KEYS - 12
     3   UTILITIES     - PERFORM SPF UTILITY FUNCTIONS
     4   FOREGROUND    - COMPILE, ASSEMBLE, LINK EDIT, OR DEBUG
     5   BACKGROUND    - COMPILE, ASSEMBLE, OR LINK EDIT
     6   COMMAND       - ENTER TSO COMMAND OR CLIST
     7   SUPPORT       - TEST DIALOG OR CONVERT MENU/MESSAGE FORMATS
     T   TUTORIAL      - DISPLAY INFORMATION ABOUT SPF
     X   EXIT          - TERMINATE SPF USING LIST/LOG DEFAULTS

     PRESS END KEY TO TERMINATE SPF
```

Figure 6.3. Going to the editor.

```
                           ┌───────────────────┐
                           │ Key in dataset name │
                           └───────────────────┘
     ----------------EDIT ENTRY PANEL -----------------------------
     ENTER/VERIFY PARAMETERS BELOW:

     SPF LIBRARY:
        PROJECT ===>
        LIBRARY ===>
        TYPE    ===>
        MEMBER  ===>            (BLANK FOR MEMBER SELECTION LIST)

     OTHER PARTITIONED OR SEQUENTIAL DATASET:
        DATASET NAME  ===> REXXPGM.EXEC
        VOLUME SERIAL ===>            (IF NOT CATALOGUED)
     DATASET PASSWORD ===>            (IF PASSWORD PROTECTED)
     PROFILE NAME     ===>            (BLANK DEFAULTS TO DATASET TYPE)
```

Figure 6.4. Editor entry panel.

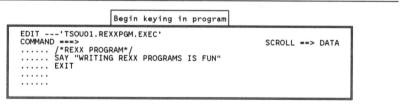

```
                           ┌────────────────────────┐
                           │ Begin keying in program │
                           └────────────────────────┘
     EDIT ---'TSOU01.REXXPGM.EXEC'
     COMMAND ===>                              SCROLL ==> DATA
     ...... /*REXX PROGRAM*/
     ...... SAY "WRITING REXX PROGRAMS IS FUN"
     ...... EXIT
     ......
     ......
```

Figure 6.5. Keying in the program inside the editor.

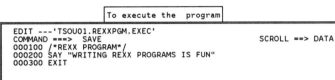

```
                          To execute the  program
EDIT ---'TSOU01.REXXPGM.EXEC'
COMMAND ===>   SAVE                              SCROLL ==> DATA
000100 /*REXX PROGRAM*/
000200 SAY "WRITING REXX PROGRAMS IS FUN"
000300 EXIT
```

Figure 6.6. Saving the program before executing it.

```
                              then ....
EDIT ---'TSOU01.REXXPGM.EXEC'
COMMAND ===>   TSO EXEC REXXPGM EXEC            SCROLL ==> DATA
000100 /*REXX PROGRAM*/
000200 SAY "WRITING REXX PROGRAMS IS FUN"
000300 EXIT
```

Figure 6.7. Executing the program while still in the editor.

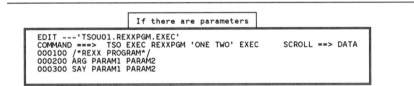

```
                          If there are parameters
EDIT ---'TSOU01.REXXPGM.EXEC'
COMMAND ===>   TSO EXEC REXXPGM 'ONE TWO' EXEC    SCROLL ==> DATA
000100 /*REXX PROGRAM*/
000200 ARG PARAM1 PARAM2
000300 SAY PARAM1 PARAM2
```

Figure 6.8. Executing the program while still in the editor, passing two parameters to the program.

```
                      If a parameter needs apostrophes
EDIT ---'TSOU01.REXXPGM.EXEC'
COMMAND ===>   TSO EXEC REXXPGM ' ''ONE'' TWO' EXEC  SCROLL ==> DATA
000100 /*REXX PROGRAM*/
000200 ARG PARAM1 PARAM2
000300 SAY PARAM1 PARAM2
```

Figure 6.9. Executing the program while still in the editor, passing two parameters to the program: the first one needs apostrophes.

6.3 QUESTIONS/PROBLEMS

Problem 6.1: Create a Sequential REXX Exec named LISTER.EXEC.
Place in it these TSO commands:
    LISTCAT
    LISTDS LISTER.EXEC

Chapter 7

HOW TO CREATE AND EXECUTE A PARTITIONED REXX EXEC

This chapter will show you step-by-step how you should create and execute a REXX program contained in a partitioned dataset, or library. If you have been creating and executing partitioned CLISTs you should have no difficulty here, and may even skip this chapter if you wish.

If, on the other hand, you have never created a REXX program or a CLIST, you may want to follow the steps shown in this chapter from start to finish.

Topics:

7.1 Creating a Partitioned Exec
7.2 Executing a Partitioned Exec
7.3 Executing the Partitioned Exec

7.1 CREATING A PARTITIONED EXEC

Follow these steps one after another, to create and execute a Partitioned REXX program. There may be other ways of doing this that are just as good, but if you follow these steps you're sure to wind up with a usable program.

I'm assuming you are using ISPF in your installation. ISPF has an excellent editor, and a panel for creating datasets. If you aren't already in ISPF, go into it now. Your installation manager can show you how, but generally you just type in "ISPF" after logging on to TSO.

Choose Option 3.2, from the ISPF main menu, or Primary Options Panel. You should now be looking at something like Figure 7.1. If you aren't, ask someone how to get to the Dataset Utility Allocate panel.

There are two things to type in on this panel.

"A" for Allocate in the SELECT OPTION field, and the name of your program in the field DATASET NAME. The only requirement here for a

REXX program, is that the name end in .EXEC. Please note that this is not an absolute requirement. I have entered the name REXXPRGS.EXEC on the panel in Figure 7.1. I will assume that this is the name of your program library in this and many more examples in this book. Now press ENTER.

You should now see something like Figure 7.2. It is very likely that the attributes shown on your screen will not be the ones you see here. This is no problem. Just type over them, changing them to what you see here.

These attributes should be used if your installation does not have standards for them. Volume Serial and Generic Unit are very much installation dependant. Ask someone what to type in here. If you can't find anyone, you can usually omit Volume Serial, and TSO will accommodatingly supply a Volume Serial number. As for Generic Unit, if your installation requires you to specify something here, you will have to find out what that is. If you guess, you may find yourself with a program on an illegal disk pack, and someone may delete it on you. The field DIRECTORY BLOCKS needs an explanation. If you put a zero or blank here, you get a sequential dataset, not a library. We do want a library, so we'll have to put something here. Each directory block can hold at least four members, or individual programs. I suggest you type "10" here, as this will allow you to place forty programs into your program library. Press ENTER. You should see the message "Dataset Allocated" in the upper right of your screen.

Now let's go into the library we have allocated and key in the lines of our program (see Figure 7.3). From the Main Menu, or Primary Option Panel, choose option 2, the ISPF editor.

Figure 7.4 shows the editor entry panel. It needs only one piece of information, the name of the library you allocated in previous steps. Key it in the fields "PROJECT", "LIBRARY", and "TYPE", as shown. Notice how that's done. Your userid, TSOU01 in the example, goes in the "PROJECT" field. The second part of the library name, which is REXXPRGS in my example, goes in the field "LIBRARY". The third part of the library name, which should be EXEC, goes in the field "TYPE". You have to key a name in the "MEMBER" field, since this is the first time you are editing this library. The next time you edit it, you won't have to key in a member name. ISPF will then present you with a list of members. I have used the member name MYFIRST here. You may use any other name you want. I hope this isn't your first time using the ISPF editor. If you haven't used it before, this is the time to look for my book on TSO and ISPF, "MVS/TSO: Mastering Native Mode and ISPF", QED March 1990. Press ENTER.

Now you're in the editor, and should be looking at a panel like Figure 7.5, except that your program won't have been keyed in just yet. That's what you'll do now. Reminder: the comment goes first, and columns are not significant with REXX. I suggest one statement or instruction per line.

When you're satisfied that your program looks good, you can save it and execute it (see Figure 7.6). Type SAVE on the command line, and press ENTER.

7.2 EXECUTING A PARTITIONED EXEC.

We'll show you how to execute your program while you're still in the editor. This makes it easier for you to correct your program when the inevitable mishap occurs, because you will never leave the editor, and so will not have to go back into the editor.

Type the command in the command line area, as shown in Figure 7.7. The command to execute your program (if no concatenation was done) is TSO EXEC program-name EXEC. The TSO is required, since you are still in ISPF, and you need to prefix line mode TSO commands with "TSO" in order to execute them. The first EXEC tells TSO to look at this as a CLIST or REXX exec to be executed. Next you place your program name. You do not need the full name of your program, just the middle part and member name, minus your userid, and minus the EXEC part of the name. Last you specify EXEC once again. This is needed so TSO will know that you are executing a REXX program, not a CLIST.

Figure 7.8 assumes no concatenation was done. If your REXX program needs to have parameters passed to it at execution time, you may do it this way. Place them all within one set of apostrophes. The apostrophes are not passed to your program. They are needed so TSO knows there are parameters.

Figure 7.9 also assumes no concatenation was done. It's possible that one of the parameters needs apostrophes around it. This usually occurs with dataset names, since TSO requires apostrophes around dataset names that do not belong to you. If a parameter needs apostrophes, you have to double those apostrophes. This means two consecutive apostrophes, not the quotation mark. The double apostrophes are changed to single ones and passed to your program as single apostrophes. So the parameter ONE in this panel, would appear in your program as 'ONE'. Reminder: the apostrophe after REXXPRGS and the one after TWO are there because this manner of executing programs requires apostrophes if there are parameters.

You will most likely have done the concatenation suggested in the next chapter (see Figure 7.10). This will allow you to execute your program in what I feel is a more convenient manner. You simply type in "TSO" (since you are still in ISPF, and this is a TSO command) a space, a percent sign and your program member name in the library. Since your program's member name is MYFIRST, you'll have to type in TSO %MYFIRST to execute your program.

Figure 7.11 assumes concatenation was done. This is how you execute if your program needs parameters. Please notice that there are no apostrophes used. This method of execution, with percent sign and the member name, does not require apostrophes when there are parameters. I think this is a more natural method than the one used with sequential programs, and the method used in Figures 7.8 and 7.9. This is why I hope you'll do the concatenation described in the next chapter.

Figure 7.12 also assumes concatenation was done. When one of the parameters needs apostrophes, you simply type in the apostrophes as you would have done if this were an ordinary TSO command. No doubling is needed.

```
                              ┌─ ISPF 3.2 ─┐
─────────────────────────────DATASET UTILITY ─────────────────────────
SELECT OPTION ===> A

   A - ALLOCATE NEW DATASET              C - CATALOG DATASET
   R - RENAME ENTIRE DATASET             U - UNCATALOG DATASET
   D - DELETE ENTIRE DATASET

   BLANK - DISPLAY DATASET INFORMATION

SPF LIBRARY
   PROJECT ===>
   LIBRARY ===>
   TYPE    ===>

OTHER PARTITIONED OR SEQUENTIAL DATASET
   DATASET NAME   ===> REXXPRGS.EXEC
   VOLUME SERIAL ===>       (IF NOT CATALOGUED, REQUIRED FOR OPTION "C")
```

Figure 7.1. Dataset Utility Allocate panel.

```
                    ┌─ Allocate using ISPF utility ─┐
──────────────ALLOCATE NEW DATASET ───────────────────────────
DATASET NAME 'TSOU01.REXXPRGS.EXEC'

   VOLUME SERIAL      ===>       (BLANK FOR AUTHORIZED DEFAULT VOLUME)
   GENERIC UNIT       ===>
   SPACE UNITS        ===> TRKS  (BLKS, TRKS, OR CYLS)
   PRIMARY QUANTITY   ===> 10    (IN ABOVE UNITS)
   SECONDARY QUAN     ===> 5     (IN ABOVE UNITS)
   DIRECTORY BLOCKS   ===> 10    (ZERO FOR SEQUENTIAL DATASET)
   RECORD FORMAT      ===> FB
   RECORD LENGTH      ===> 80
   BLOCK SIZE         ===> 6240
```

Figure 7.2. Dataset Allocate Attribute Panel.

```
                              ┌──────────────┐
                              │ Choose EDIT  │
                              └──────────────┘
                              SPF-MVS PRIMARY OPTION MENU
 SELECT OPTION ===> 2
              -
 O  SPF PARMS    - SPECIFY TERMINAL AND SPF PARAMETERS   TIME 11:06
 1  BROWSE       - DISPLAY SOURCE DATA OR OUTPUT LISTINGS TERMINAL 3278
 2  EDIT         - CREATE OR CHANGE SOURCE DATA             PF KEYS - 12
 3  UTILITIES    - PERFORM SPF UTILITY FUNCTIONS
 4  FOREGROUND   - COMPILE, ASSEMBLE, LINK EDIT, OR DEBUG
 5  BACKGROUND   - COMPILE, ASSEMBLE, OR LINK EDIT
 6  COMMAND      - ENTER TSO COMMAND OR CLIST
 7  SUPPORT      - TEST DIALOG OR CONVERT MENU/MESSAGE FORMATS
 T  TUTORIAL     - DISPLAY INFORMATION ABOUT SPF
 X  EXIT         - TERMINATE SPF USING LIST/LOG DEFAULTS

 PRESS END KEY TO TERMINATE SPF
```

Figure 7.3. Choosing EDIT from the Main Menu, or Primary Option Panel.

```
                         ┌──────────────────────────────┐
                         │ Key in dataset name and member name │
                         └──────────────────────────────┘
 -----------------EDIT ENTRY PANEL -----------------------------
 ENTER/VERIFY PARAMETERS BELOW:

 SPF LIBRARY:
     PROJECT ===> TSOU01
     LIBRARY ===> REXXPRGS
     TYPE    ===> EXEC
     MEMBER  ===> MYFIRST    (BLANK FOR MEMBER SELECTION LIST)

 OTHER PARTITIONED OR SEQUENTIAL DATASET:
     DATASET NAME   ===>
     VOLUME SERIAL ===>                (IF NOT CATALOGUED)
 DATASET PASSWORD ===>                (IF PASSWORD PROTECTED)
 PROFILE NAME      ===>                (BLANK DEFAULTS TO DATASET TYPE)
```

Figure 7.4. Keying in the name of your program library, and a new member name on the EDIT entry panel.

```
                         ┌────────────────────────┐
                         │ Begin keying in program │
                         └────────────────────────┘
 EDIT ---'TSOU01.REXXPRGS.EXEC(MYFIRST)'
 COMMAND ===>                            SCROLL ==> DATA
 ...... /*REXX PROGRAM*/
 ...... SAY "WRITING REXX PROGRAMS IS FUN"
 ...... EXIT
 ...... /* 1990 G.F.Gargiulo */
 ......
```

Figure 7.5. Keying in the program in the editor.

7.3 EXECUTING THE PROGRAM, EXAMPLES.

```
                     ┌─────────────────────────┐
                     │ To execute the  program │
     ┌───────────────┴─────────────────────────┴──────────────────┐
     │ EDIT ---'TSOU01.REXXPRGS.EXEC(MYFIRST)'                     │
     │ COMMAND ===>  SAVE                        SCROLL ==> DATA    │
     │ 000100 /*REXX PROGRAM*/                                     │
     │ 000200 SAY "WRITING REXX PROGRAMS IS FUN"                   │
     │ 000300 EXIT                                                 │
     │ 000400 /* 1990 G.F.Gargiulo */                             │
     └────────────────────────────────────────────────────────────┘
```

Figure 7.6. Saving the program while still in the editor.

```
                     ┌─────────────────────────┐
                     │        then ....        │
     ┌───────────────┴─────────────────────────┴──────────────────┐
     │ EDIT ---'TSOU01.REXXPRGS.EXEC(MYFIRST)'                     │
     │ COMMAND ===>  TSO EXEC REXXPRGS(MYFIRST) EXEC   SCROLL ==> DATA │
     │ 000100 /*REXX PROGRAM*/                                     │
     │ 000200 SAY "WRITING REXX PROGRAMS IS FUN"                   │
     │ 000300 EXIT                                                 │
     │ 000400 /* 1990 G.F.Gargiulo                        */       │
     └────────────────────────────────────────────────────────────┘
```

Figure 7.7. Executing the program while still in the editor.

```
                     ┌─────────────────────────┐
                     │   If there are parameters │
     ┌───────────────┴─────────────────────────┴──────────────────┐
     │ EDIT ---'TSOU01.REXXPRGS.EXEC(MYFIRST)'                     │
     │ COMMAND ===>  TSO EXEC REXXPRGS(MYFIRST) 'ONE TWO' EXEC  SCROLL │
     │ 000100 /*REXX PROGRAM*/                                     │
     │ 000200 ARG PARAM1 PARAM2                                    │
     │ 000300 SAY PARAM1 PARAM2                                    │
     │ 000400 /* 1990 G.F.Gargiulo                        */       │
     └────────────────────────────────────────────────────────────┘
```

Figure 7.8. Executing the program while still in the editor, two parameters are required by the program.

```
                     ┌─────────────────────────────────────┐
                     │  If a parameter needs apostrophes    │
┌────────────────────┴─────────────────────────────────────┴────────────────┐
│ EDIT ---'TSOU01.REXXPRGS.EXEC(MYFIRST)'                                     │
│ COMMAND ==> TSO EXEC REXXPRGS(MYFIRST) ' ''ONE'' TWO' EXEC      SCROL       │
│ 000100 /*REXX PROGRAM*/                                                     │
│ 000200 ARG PARAM1 PARAM2                                                    │
│ 000300 SAY PARAM1 PARAM2                                                    │
│ 000400 /* 1990 G.F.Gargiulo                                     */          │
│                                                                            │
└────────────────────────────────────────────────────────────────────────────┘
```

Figure 7.9. Executing the program while still in the editor, two parameters are required by the program, one of the parameters needs apostrophes around it.

```
                     ┌─────────────────────────────────────┐
                     │            If concat done            │
┌────────────────────┴─────────────────────────────────────┴────────────────┐
│ EDIT ---'TSOU01.REXXPRGS.EXEC(MYFIRST)'                                     │
│ COMMAND ===>  TSO   %myfirst                          SCROLL ==> DATA       │
│ 000100 /*REXX PROGRAM*/                                                     │
│ 000200 SAY "WRITING REXX PROGRAMS IS FUN"                                   │
│ 000300 EXIT                                                                 │
│ 000400 /* 1990 G.F.Gargiulo                                     */          │
│                                                                            │
└────────────────────────────────────────────────────────────────────────────┘
```

Figure 7.10. Executing the program while still in the editor. The concatenation described in the next chapter has been done.

```
                     ┌─────────────────────────────────────┐
                     │        If there are parameters       │
┌────────────────────┴─────────────────────────────────────┴────────────────┐
│ EDIT ---'TSOU01.REXXPRGS.EXEC(MYFIRST)'                                     │
│ COMMAND ===>   TSO %myfirst one two                            SCROLL       │
│ 000100 /*REXX PROGRAM*/                                                     │
│ 000200 ARG PARAM1 PARAM2                                                    │
│ 000300 SAY PARAM1 PARAM2                                                    │
│ 000400 /* 1990 G.F.Gargiulo                                     */          │
│                                                                            │
└────────────────────────────────────────────────────────────────────────────┘
```

Figure 7.11. Executing the program while still in the editor. Concatenation has been done. The program requires two parameters.

```
                         ┌─────────────────────────────────┐
                         │ If a parameter needs apostrophes │
 ┌───────────────────────┴─────────────────────────────────┴──────────┐
 │ EDIT ---'TSOU01.REXXPRGS.EXEC(MYFIRST)'                             │
 │ COMMAND ==> TSO %myfirst 'one' two                      SCROL       │
 │ 000100 /*REXX PROGRAM*/                                             │
 │ 000200 ARG PARAM1 PARAM2                                            │
 │ 000300 SAY PARAM1 PARAM2                                            │
 │ 000400 /* 1990 G.F.Gargiulo                             */          │
 │                                                                     │
 └─────────────────────────────────────────────────────────────────────┘
```

Figure 7.12. Executing the program while still in the editor. The concatenation described in the next chapter has been done. The program requires two parameters, and the first parameter needs apostrophes.

Chapter 8

CONCATENATING YOUR PARTITIONED REXX EXEC

This chapter gives you all the information you'll need to run any programs in your program library by just typing in their member name. Your installation may very well have written some instructions that will do everything in this chapter for you! I hope that is true in your case. But even if you have to do all this for yourself, take consolation in the knowledge that you'll have to do it only once.

In this chapter I'll tell you why concatenating is so important, and, of course, how to do it. Then I'll tell you how to create an exec that will do the concatenating for you. Last, I'll have you put the name of that exec on your Logon Screen, to have TSO automatically execute it every time you log on. TSO will also keep that name on your Logon Screen, so you won't have to key it in again.

Topics:

8.1 Why Concatenate?
8.2 What the Concatenate Command looks like
8.3 Will you use SYSEXEC or SYSPROC?
8.4 If SYSEXEC doesn't work
8.5 Concatenation: Step-by-Step
8.6 Questions/Problems

8.1 WHY CONCATENATE?

TSO will look in any library that is allocated to the DDNAME SYSEXEC to find REXX programs. It will also look in any library that is allocated to the DDNAME SYSPROC to find CLISTs and/or REXX programs. Concatenation means specifying more than one library in the ALLOCATE command. This means that TSO will search through all the libraries that are specified in order to find a program. Concatenating is like adding your own private command library to TSO's.

Concatenating gives you the ability to create and use custom functions and/or subroutines, to create and use EDIT macros, and to use custom functions in QMF (Query Management Facility). Finally, concatenation allows you to execute your program in a very simple manner (see Figure 8.1). You simply put a percent sign before the program's member name in its library, and type it in. The percent sign is in fact optional, but it gives you more efficiency in executing your program. I recommend you get in the habit of always prefixing your program's name with a percent sign. No one will force you to concatenate, but if you don't, you'll have to execute your program as shown in Figure 8.2, and you won't be able to use custom functions.

```
%FIRSTONE   ONE TWO
```

Figure 8.1. How you can execute if you concatenate.

```
EXEC REXXPRGS(FIRSTONE) 'ONE TWO'
```

Figure 8.2. How you must execute if you don't concatenate.

8.2 WHAT THE CONCATENATE COMMAND LOOKS LIKE

In Figure 8.3 I show you what the concatenate command looks like. You may know enough about TSO in your installation to just create this command and type it in without doing everything that is shown in this chapter. This command is what we're aiming for in this chapter, and because there are so many steps involved, I'm including it here so you can keep it in mind as you do everything needed to create it.

Notice the hyphen at the end of the first line. You may omit the hyphen if you type in the whole command, both lines, in one continuous string of characters, as a one line command.

The major part of this chapter is concerned with finding out which names to use for first-exec-pds, and second-exec-pds.

```
ALLOCATE DDNAME(SYSEXEC) SHR REUSE -
DSNAME(first-exec-pds second-exec-pds..-
                            your-exec-pds)
```

Figure 8.3. The concatenate command we will need to do.

8.3 WILL YOU USE SYSEXEC OR SYSPROC?

The sample command I've shown you in Figure 8.3 uses the DDNAME SYSEXEC. Normally SYSEXEC is what you should use, because TSO will search the libraries allocated to SYSEXEC before it searches libraries allocated to SYSPROC. Please plan on using SYSEXEC, unless your installation prefers that you use SYSPROC. If so, please substitute SYSPROC for SYSEXEC in what follows. Everything will still work as it should.

8.4 IF SYSEXEC DOESN'T WORK

If you have used SYSEXEC and done everything right, it is nevertheless possible that TSO still won't be able to find your REXX programs. You may see the message "Command not found". This means that your installation hasn't activated the DDNAME SYSEXEC. It means that when your REXX interpreter was installed, it was not told to search the DDNAME SYSEXEC. No problem. Just execute the command shown in Figure 8.4. This tells TSO to search in the DDNAME SYSEXEC. You'll have to do this command each time you log on. You may also put it into the setup exec we recommend at the end of this chapter.

There is no problem if you execute this command and don't need to. It just won't do anything.

```
EXECUTIL SEARCHDD(YES)
```

Figure 8.4. Command that will activate SYSEXEC.

8.5 CONCATENATING: STEP BY STEP

The next several steps will enable you to do the concatenation you need to do, and to create a setup exec that will make your future TSO sessions so much easier.

Please note that Appendix D contains an exec that will automate these steps.

1. Execute the LISTALC command shown in Figure 8.5. This will display the names of datasets that your TSO session is currently using. There will be a lengthy display. Watch for the DDNAME SYSEXEC in the display. You should be in line mode, or Native TSO.

2. Inspect the output displayed by the above command. If you see the name SYSEXEC, write down the name of the dataset just above it, and the names of the datasets after it, until you come to another DDNAME.

In the sample display in Figure 8.6, the dataset 'SYSTEM.REXXEXCS.EXEC' and the dataset 'GROUP.REXXPGMS.EXEC' are both allocated to the DDNAME SYSEXEC. Please notice that the datasets 'AREA.PROCS.CLIST' and 'GROUP.PROCS.CLIST' are allocated to the DDNAME SYSPROC in this example.

3. Write down the name, or names of datasets that are allocated to SYSEXEC in your TSO session (see Figure 8.7). There may be none. If there are none, just do not write down any names.

4. This step is optional. If everything works well you may decide to skip it. The attributes shown in Chapter 7 should work in most installations. But if they don't work, you'll see the error message "System abend 001", and your program will terminate.

Please check the attributes of the first library that you wrote down, and compare them to the attributes of the library that you allocated in Chapter 7. Type in the following command:

> LISTDS first library-name
> For Example:
> LISTDS 'SYSTEM.REXXEXCS.EXEC'

Write down the attributes shown:
Record Length___ Block Size___ Record Format ___

Do the same command for your REXX program library,

>For Example:
>LISTDS 'TSOU01.REXXPRGS.EXEC'

Write down the attributes shown:
Record Length___ Block Size___ Record Format ___
If both libraries have the same attributes all is well. Otherwise you may get the System abend message shown above, and you'll have to go back and reallocate your REXX program library with the same attributes as those of the first library.

5. Write down in Figure 8.8 the names of libraries that you wrote in Figure 8.7. If the names don't belong to you (they probably won't), write them with apostrophes around them. Write them in the same order that they were in Figure 8.7. You should have something like what you see in Figure 8.9.

6. Using Figure 8.10 as a sample, write down the name of your REXX program library, in the last space in Figure 8.8. Since it is your library, you don't need to specify it with apostrophes.

7. You now have something that looks like Figure 8.11. You can type it in. Executing this command will do the actual allocation with concatenation.

Many things can go wrong at this point:

* You may need to exit from ISPF in order to do this command.
* Your installation may have done an allocation at logon time that you cannot change.
* You may have incorrectly noted one of the dataset names.
* Your command syntax may be wrong. (You don't need the hyphens shown if you type in the command in one continuous string. Don't press ENTER until the end.)

8. If everything appears to have worked, do another LISTALC STATUS command, and see if it did. The output of your LISTALC STATUS command should show your REXX program library as the last of the datasets allocated to SYSEXEC. Note the arrow in Figure 8.12.

9. This step is optional, but if you want to cut down on your typing, and get to a point where you can be productive more quickly, I recommend you do it (see Figure 8.13).

You are creating an exec that will do the command that you created as a result of following the steps in this chapter. I suggest you name this exec SETUP, and place it in your REXX program library. That means that its full name will be, for example REXXPRGS.EXEC(SETUP). I have shown it with the command EXECUTIL. This command activates the DDNAME SYSEXEC, in case it wasn't already done. It won't hurt at all if you include this command and don't need it. You might notice that I included the keyword REUSE in my ALLOCATE command. This allows you to do the

ALLOCATE command without doing a FREE first.

The commas at the end of the second and third lines are REXX's way of continuing long commands onto another line. You will need to use them as shown.

10. The next time you log on, key in the name of your setup exec in the COMMAND field of the Logon panel (see Figure 8.14). This tells TSO to execute your setup exec everytime you log on. That way you won't have to type in this setup exec again, and your concatenation will be done automatically every time you log on.

Sometimes you'll get this far having done everything correctly and your setup exec still won't work! This is because some installations have already told TSO to execute a command at logon time. They have specified a command in the Logon Procedure for TSO. You can't change that, and you can't override it. It means that you should not type your setup exec on the Logon panel.

```
LISTALC STATUS
```

Figure 8.5. LISTALC command.

```
LISTALC STATUS

DDNAME --- DISP

dataset name

ddname      KEEP


ABC.TEST.DATA

INFILE      KEEP

SYSTEM.REXXEXCS.EXEC

SYSEXEC     KEEP

GROUP.REXXPGMS.EXEC

            KEEP


AREA.PROCS.CLIST

SYSPROC     KEEP

GROUP.PROCS.CLIST

            KEEP
```

Figure 8.6. Possible result of a LISTALC STATUS.

Figure 8.7. Space for you to write down the result of your LISTDS command.

```
ALLOCATE DDNAME(SYSEXEC) SHR REUSE -
DSNAME(                                              -
                                                      )
```

Figure 8.8. Space for you to write in the names of datasets currently allocated to the DDNAME SYSEXEC.

```
ALLOCATE DDNAME(SYSEXEC) SHR REUSE -
DSNAME('SYSTEM.REXXEXCS.EXEC'  'GROUP.REXXPGMS.EXEC'  -
                                    your-exec-pds)
```

Figure 8.9. Example of the command you might have created based on your LISTALC STATUS.

```
ALLOCATE DDNAME(SYSEXEC) SHR REUSE -
DSNAME('SYSTEM.REXXEXCS.EXEC'  'GROUP.REXXPGMS.EXEC'  -
                    REXXPRGS.EXEC                )
```

Figure 8.10. Example of the command you might have created based on your LISTALC STATUS, with a sample REXX program library included (REXXPRGS.EXEC).

```
ALLOCATE DDNAME(SYSEXEC) SHR REUSE -
DSNAME('SYSTEM.REXXEXCS.EXEC'  'GROUP.REXXPGMS.EXEC'  -
                    REXXPRGS.EXEC                )
```

Figure 8.11. Example of a possible command that one may need to type in in order to do a concatenation. Type it in on one line, omitting the hyphens.

```
LISTALC STATUS

    DDNAME --- DISP

    ABC.TEST.DATA
    INFILE      KEEP
    SYSTEM.REXXEXCS.EXEC
    SYSEXEC     KEEP
    GROUP.REXXPGMS.EXEC
                KEEP
    TSOU01.REXXPRGS.EXEC <-------------
                KEEP
    AREA.PROCS.CLIST
    SYSPROC     KEEP
    GROUP.PROCS.CLIST
                KEEP
```

Figure 8.12. Possible result of a LISTALC STATUS after concatenating your Exec library to SYSEXEC.

```
/*REXX EXEC TO SETUP CONCATENATION.
           NAMED REXXPRGS.EXEC(SETUP)*/
"EXECUTIL SEARCHDD(YES)"
"ALLOCATE DDNAME(SYSEXEC) SHR REUSE ",
"DSNAME('SYSTEM.REXXEXCS.EXEC' 'GROUP.REXXPGMS.EXEC'",
"                         REXXPRGS.EXEC      ) "
```

Figure 8.13. Example of a Setup exec that will make it easier to concatenate your program library when you log on.

```
----------------------------TSO/E LOGON --------------------------
PF1/PF13 => Help  PF3/PF15 => Logoff  PA1 => Attention PA2 => Reshow
You may request specific HELP info by entering '?' in any entry field
  ENTER LOGON PARAMETERS BELOW:              RACF LOGON PARAMETERS:

  USERID    ===> TSOU01

  PASSWORD  ===>                    NEW PASSWORD ===>

  PROCEDURE ===> TSOPROC1          GROUP IDENT  ===>

  ACCT NMBR ===> 12345

  SIZE      ===>

  PERFORM   ===>

  COMMAND   ===> EXEC REXXPRGS(SETUP)  EXEC

  ENTER AN 'S' BEFORE EACH OPTION DESIRED BELOW:
    __NOMAIL      __NONOTICE       __RECONNECT     __OIDCARD
```

Figure 8.14. The TSO/E logon panel showing the name of the setup exec of Figure 8.13 keyed in the COMMAND field.

8.6 QUESTIONS/PROBLEMS

Q 8.1: How many directory blocks do you allocate for a sequential Exec dataset?

Q 8.2: How many directory blocks do you allocate for a partitioned Exec dataset that will contain 30 members?

Problem 8.3: After doing the allocation and concatenation described in this chapter, create an exec named TRYIT, containing this command:
      SAY "THIS IS THE TRYIT EXEC"
Execute it this way: %TRYIT.

Chapter 9

SIMPLIFIED SYNTAX

In this chapter I'd like to acquaint you with the syntax of REXX, its grammatical components. You need to know something about REXX's syntax in order to avoid frequent syntax error messages. I've found that you don't need to know a lot in order to write correct REXX programs. Consequently, I've simplified the syntax of REXX to save you time in learning it. However, some of the details of REXX syntax may be of interest to you, and so I'll send you to the authority on the subject, Michael F. Cowlishaw's book "The REXX Language" Prentice Hall, Englewood Cliffs N.J. 1985.

Topics:

9.1 Fundamentals
9.2 Components of REXX
9.3 Questions/Problems

9.1 FUNDAMENTALS

Look at Figure 9.1 in reference to the following comments:

Line 1 - The first thing that will strike you about a REXX program, is that it is always started with a comment. In the TSO environment, this comment must contain the word REXX, so as to distinguish it from a CLIST. I suggest you start all your REXX execs this way.

Line 1 - You may place comments anywhere in your program. Generally you should place them in such a way that they don't impede readability. This generally means on a line by themselves, or off to the right of an instruction.
    Your comment may carry over to several lines. In that case, you may end the comment on a line other than the one it started with.

```
1 /*REXX program.........*/
2 SAY "HELLO"
3 Say "GOODBYE"
4 A = 5
5 SAY "HELLO";SAY "GOODBYE"
6 SAY "HELLO";
7 SAY,
8 "HELLO"
```

Figure 9.1. Sample REXX statements.

Lines 2, 3, 4 - I suggest you put one statement on a line. This makes for a program that is easier to read. Athough it is legal to say SAY "HELLO";SAY "GOODBYE", I think it is generally better to avoid that.

Line 3 - You may use upper and lower case as convenient, except when literals are being compared, where upper and lower case is significant.

Line 4 - The assignment statement has no verb. It is variable = value.

Line 5 - If you want to place more than one instruction on a line, you'll have to use the semicolon. This is generally not recommended, however.

Line 6 - If nothing follows, on the same line, the semicolon is not needed. I suggest you not use it, when there is nothing else on the line, since it adds nothing to readability.

Lines 7, 8 - Generally one instruction or statement occupies one line of your program. However, you may sometimes need to use two or more lines. When this happens, simply end the first line with a comma. This tells REXX to take this line together with the next. For example, normally SAY and "HELLO" should be on the same line. However if you wanted to use two lines for this one instruction, you would leave a comma at the end of the first line.

9.2 COMPONENTS OF REXX

I have broken REXX down, somewhat arbitrarily, into six components: keywords, the assignment statement, the literal, the variable, the command, and the label (see Figures 9.2 and 9.3).

The keyword.

Like most languages, REXX has verbs, with a specific meaning. Each verb is a keyword and is found first in the sentence. There are not many different REXX keywords, and you will learn them in this book.

The assignment statement.

This is recognized by its second component, the equal sign. The first component is a variable, and may not be in quotes. The variable is made equal to whatever is to the right of the equal sign.

The literal.

The literal is itself. It stands for nothing else. Normally, literals are enclosed in quotes or apostrophes, in REXX. I recommend you always enclose literals in quotes or apostrophes, although REXX can interpret a literal as such if you forget the quotes or apostrophes. REXX will first look to see if the string of characters is a variable. If it is a variable, then REXX uses the contents of the variable. If it is not a variable, then REXX takes the character string as a literal, but will convert it to uppercase. I recommend you not make use of this feature, but it is handy when you forget the quotes or apostrophes.

The variable.

The variable holds information. It represents the information, which may change during the course of execution of the program.

The command.

I will use the word "command" to mean something that REXX doesn't understand, and that it passes to TSO for TSO to process. More on this later, in the chapter "Talking to the Environment". For now, I'd just like to say that your commands should be enclosed in quotes or apostrophes.

The label.

A label is used to name a subroutine, user-written function, an error trap, or is the target of a transfer of control instruction. A label must be the first thing on the line, and end with a colon. The label may also be alone on the line.

Keyword	assignment	literal	variable	command
SAY	A = 5	"HELLO"	A	ALLOCATE
IF		'GOODBYE'	B	DELETE
DO		HELLO	C	LOGOFF
EXIT		12345	NAME	
		'12345'		

Figure 9.2. Some components of REXX.

```
COMPUTE:  C = A + B

COMPUTE:
   C = A + B
```

Figure 9.3. The label.

9.3 QUESTIONS/PROBLEMS

Q 9.1: Are these correct syntax?

1 SAY "HELLO";SAY "GOODBYE"

2 SAY "HELLO";
  SAY;
  "GOODBYE"

3 COMPUTE;   C = 3 + 4

Q 9.2: A label is the target of an instruction that transfers control to it. T/F.

Q 9.3: The instruction EXIT must always be the very last line in the program. T/F

Q 9.4: Will REXX try to execute this line?
       BARK "HELLO"

Problem 9.5: Write an Exec to execute the TSO commands:

    TIME
    Send 'sample Exec ' user(*)

Include the comment:
       This is a sample Exec for REXX class
Execute the REXX command:
       Say TIME() DATE()
But use two lines and a continuation character.
Expected results:

    = = > %p0905
    09:05:02 03/08/42 CPU 4.3 SVC 888.323
    + SAMPLE EXEC TSOU01
    09:05:02 03/08/42

Chapter 10

THE LITERAL

This chapter is about the literal in REXX. You'll learn about using quotes and apostrophes, how to continue a literal on a second line, and a special kind of literal, the Hex string. Finally you'll see a possible pitfall that arises because of the way that REXX interprets a Hex string.

Topics:

10.1 FUNCTION OF THE LITERAL

Let's see some details about the literal in REXX. Some examples of literals are shown in Figure 10.1

We've already seen, in Chapter 9, that a literal stands for itself, and is usually bounded by quotes or apostrophes. Note that there may be a null string, or a literal containing no characters. You signify the null string by two consecutive quotes, or apostrophes. The maximum size of a literal is 251 characters. That should take care of most needs, since the maximum line length that the editor can handle is 251 characters too!

What do you do if a literal needs an apostrophe, as in the name O'Connor? You may bound the literal in quotation marks, as in "O'Connor", or you may double the apostrophes, as in 'O''Connor'. Something unusual about numeric literals in REXX is that they may have quotes or apostrophes, unlike COBOL. This means that the example in Figure 10.2 is legal in REXX. Also, if there's

51

an E in a number, the number is assumed to be in scientific notation. This shouldn't be a problem, unless you have a lot of addresses like "23E63 Street".

```
"HELLO"
'GOODBYE'
HELLO
12345
'12345'
GOODBYE
' '
```

Figure 10.1. Examples of literals.

```
A = '1'
B = '2'
C = A + B + "3"
```

Figure 10.2. Examples of legal numeric literals.

10.2 USING QUOTES

I strongly suggest you use quotes or apostrophes around your REXX literals, except for numeric literals. If you forget them, it still may work, but you may notice that REXX will convert literals without quotes or apostrophes to upper case letters.

10.3 CONTINUING LITERALS

Although a literal may be up to 251 characters long, you may not want to create a line that long. You may not continue a literal with a comma, but you may concatenate two literals to produce a longer one, as in Figure 10.3.

```
LONG_VAR = "LONG STRING OUT TO END OF LINE" ||,
           "REST OF STRING ON NEXT LINE"
```

Figure 10.3. Concatenating a long literal.

10.4 THE HEX STRING

If you put an X after a literal in quotes or apostrophes, REXX believes you have given it a Hex string. This means that you have put the Hexadecimal representation of character strings in the quotes. Valid Hexadecimal representations may use the digits 0-9 and the letters A-F (see Figure 10.4).

```
SAY 'F1F2F3F4'X
---> 1234
```

Figure 10.4. Displaying a Hex string.

10.5 A PITFALL

Anytime you put an X after a quoted string, REXX takes it as a HEX string.

```
/*not to do*/
X = 5 + 6
SAY "THE ANSWER IS "X
/* syntax error: attempts hex interpretation*/
```

Figure 10.5. Example of a pitfall in using literal strings.

10.6 QUESTIONS/PROBLEMS

Q 10.1: What does this program do?

```
/*TRY ME*/
SAY GREETING
```

Q 10.2: What does this program do?

```
/*TRY ME TOO*/
GREETING = "HELLO"
SAY GREETING
```

Q 10.3: Can you tell what this does? Please try it out if you don't know.

```
/*TRY ME TOO*/
GREETING = "HAPPY HALLOWEEN"
SAY GREETING
DROP GREETING
SAY GREETING
```

Q 10.4: What does this display on the screen?

```
SAY 'F2F3F4'X
```

Problem 10.5: Write an exec that displays these lines exactly as shown:

```
3 + 1 is 4
```

```
'3 + 1 is 4'
```

```
O'brien
```

Chapter 11

SAY

This chapter will concentrate on the most common and most useful REXX verb: SAY. You will see what SAY does and learn how to use it.

Topics:

11.1 Function of SAY
11.2 Questions/Problems

11.1 FUNCTION OF SAY

```
SAY "HELLO"

SAY 1 + 2
```

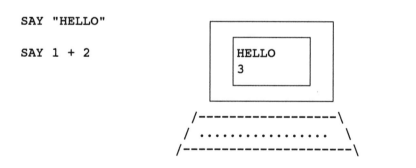

Figure 11.1. Function of SAY.

SAY displays information on the terminal screen (Figure 11.1). It displays whatever is to the right of the word SAY. If an arithmetic operation is indicated, or a concatenation, it will be performed before anything is displayed. If any one of the items displayed is a variable, the contents of the variable will be retrieved before it is displayed.

11.2 QUESTIONS/PROBLEMS

Q 11.1: What will this display on the terminal?
    SAY 5 - 3

Q 11.2: What will this display on the terminal?
    SAY "5 - 3"

Q 11.3: What will this display on the terminal?
    SAY "5" - 3

Chapter 12

THE VARIABLE

This chapter will describe the function of REXX variables, and show you how to choose names of variables correctly. It will point out several ways in which a variable receives its value.

Topics:

12.1 FUNCTION OF THE VARIABLE

A variable in REXX is very much like a variable in most other programming languages (Figure 12.1). A variable holds information, but is not the information. Each variable must be named, and each separate item of information must have a different name.

Variables are given their value through the assignment statement, the PULL, ARG, PARSE, EXECIO, and LISTDSI instructions. A variable that has never been given a value is legal, but is assumed to be equal to its name, after conversion to upper case.

12.2 VALID VARIABLES

Naming variables in REXX presents few problems. Variable names must begin with a letter, and may be as long as 250 characters. The underscore character may be used as in PLI for readability. The period is not used for readability, but is used to separate the parts of compound variables. We'll devote an entire chapter to compound variables.

Please do not use any other special character in a variable name.

A feature of REXX that makes for more readable programs, is that variable names may be upper case, lower case or mixed. I strongly suggest you avoid REXX keywords. EXIT = "HI" will work, but will also make for a very unreadable program.

12.3 UNDEFINED VARIABLES

A variable that was never given a value is taken as a literal, (but converted to uppercase) (see Figure 12.3).

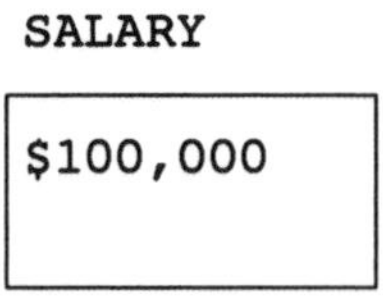

SALARY

```
$100,000
```

Figure 12.1. A variable holds information.

```
Valid Variable Names      Invalid Variable Names

A                         1        (literal number)
a                         1abccef  (begin w numb)
Aa                        a-a      (hyphen N.G)
a_A
A123
Salary_increase


Compound variable names

number.1
branch.dept.unit
A.1
```

Figure 12.2. Examples of variable names.

```
SAY Hello /*DISPLAYS "HELLO"*/
```

Figure 12.3. Displaying an undefined variable.

12.4 QUESTIONS/PROBLEMS

Q 12.1: Which variable names are invalid and why?
    A 1_time only
    B PrOgRaMmEr_nAmE
    C prog_name"
    D input-data
    E Say

Q 12.2: What does this Exec print out?
```
/*REXX exec: SHORTONE*/
MESSAGE = MESSAGE
SAY MESSAGE
EXIT
```

Problem 12.3: In an exec, assign the number 10 to a variable
assign the number 20 to another variable
in one instruction display the total of the two.

Chapter 13

CONCATENATING THINGS

This chapter will show you how to join together two or more variables or literals. It will explain how and when concatenation produces intervening blanks.

Topics:

13.1 CONCATENATING WITHOUT BLANKS

If two dissimilar items happen to be next to each other, they will be concatenated without blanks. For example, if you execute this instruction: SAY "A"5, you will see A5 displayed. The A and the 5 will be displayed without any blanks. REXX can see that they are two different items, because of the quotation marks. Other special characters will also produce this result. I suggest you not make use of this phenomenon, and that you use the concatenation operator "||" when you want two items joined (see Figure 13.2).

13.2 CONCATENATING WITH ONE BLANK

If you put two items next to each other with one or more blanks between them, one blank will remain (see Figure 13.3). Remember this rule: "One or more blanks become one blank."

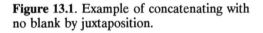

```
PERSON = "SUSAN"
SAY "HELLO"PERSON

           |
           |
           V

    HELLOSUSAN
```

Figure 13.1. Example of concatenating with no blank by juxtaposition.

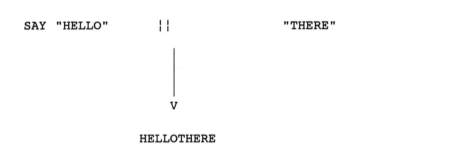

```
SAY "HELLO"        | |                "THERE"

                    |
                    |
                    V

          HELLOTHERE
```

Figure 13.2. Example of concatenating with no blank using operator.

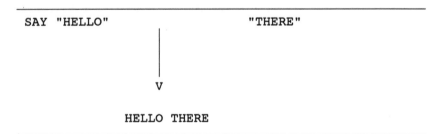

```
SAY "HELLO"                    "THERE"

               |
               |
               V

       HELLO THERE
```

Figure 13.3. Example of concatenating with a blank.

13.3 QUESTIONS/PROBLEMS

Q 13.1: When this prints out, will there be a blank
between Sam and Antha?

SAY "SAM" || "ANTHA"

Q 13.2: When this prints out, how many blanks will there be
between Kelly and Beth?

SAY "KELLY"   "BETH"

Chapter 14

IF-THE CONDITIONAL

In this chapter I'd like to acquaint you with REXX's conditional verb IF. I will also show you the unique REXX verb NOP, that does nothing. I will show you what operators you have to use if you are making more than one comparison in the same IF. I will explain how the inexact comparison works in REXX, how that is different from the ordinary comparison, and from the strictly equal comparison. Finally, I will point out what happens internally with comparisons.

Topics:

14.1 IF Syntax
14.2 Examples
14.3 Using NOP
14.4 More than one Instruction
14.5 Fuzz: the Inexact Comparison
14.6 Boolean Operators
14.7 Boolean Examples
14.8 How a Comparison becomes an Expression
14.9 Questions/Problems

14.1 IF SYNTAX

The syntax of the REXX IF does not contain many surprises (see Figure 14.1). Briefly, it is IF expression, where expression is a comparison. The expression is followed by a THEN which introduces an instruction that is executed if the comparison is true. The ELSE clause is optional, if used, it introduces an instruction which is executed if the comparison is false. You may place the IF, THEN, ELSE on separate lines, or all on the same line. I suggest you place the IF, THEN, ELSE all on separate lines.

```
IF expression
   THEN one-instruction

IF expression
   THEN one-instruction
   ELSE one-instruction

IF expression; THEN instruction;ELSE instr.
```

Figure 14.1. Possible forms of the IF.

The comparison must be expressed with a comparison operator (see Figure 14.2). You may not use words, such as EQUAL TO. REXX also uses the "not" symbol, which does not appear on all keyboards. It is the right angle symbol, used in PLI and SQL as a negation symbol. The backward slash "\" can be substituted for it.

Please note that upper and lower case are significant in REXX comparisons. This means that "Sue" is not equal to "SUE".

You may notice in Figure 14.2 that REXX has two "equal" operators, "=" and "==". There is a difference. "=" means numerically equivalent, as for example .01 and 000.010 are numerically equivalent. "=" also considers leading and trailing spaces as equivalent, so " Apples " is taken as equal to "Apples". The "strictly equal" operator, "==", means "equal in all respects." So .01 and 000.010 would not be strictly equal, and " Apples " wouldn't be strictly equal to "Apples".

`>`			greater than
`<`			less than
`/=`	`\=`	`<>`	not equal
	`==`		*really* equal, exactly the same
	`=`		numerically equivalent equivalent when padded with blanks

Figure 14.2. Comparison operators.

14.2 EXAMPLES OF IF

```
/*EXAMPLES OF IF*/
A = 1                              /*MAKE A EQUAL 1*/
IF A = 1
   THEN SAY "YES"                  /*IT SAYS YES*/


  IF A = 2
     THEN NOP
     ELSE SAY "NO"                 /*IT SAYS NO*/


IF A = 2;THEN NOP;ELSE SAY "NO" /*IT SAYS NO*/


IF A < 3
   THEN SAY "LESS THAN 3"          /*LESS THAN 3*/


NAME = "JOHN"
OTHER_NAME = "   JOHN       "


IF NAME == OTHER_NAME
   THEN SAY "STRICTLY EQUAL"
   ELSE SAY "NOT STRICTLY EQUAL"  /*NOT STRICTLY*/


IF 1.0000000 = 00000001.00
   THEN SAY "EQUAL"               /*EQUAL*/


IF 1.0000000 == 00000001.00
   THEN SAY "STRICTLY EQUAL"      /*NO!  */
   ELSE SAY "NOT STRICTLY EQUAL" /*NOT STRICTLY*/
```

Figure 14.3. Examples of the IF.

14.3 USING NOP

Sometimes you don't want to do anything at all when a condition is true, but want to do something when a condition is false. In that case, you can use the verb NOP. NOP does nothing. It is a place holder. Using NOP after ELSE is not useful, except in a nested IF, to assure that every IF has its own ELSE.

14.4 MORE THAN ONE INSTRUCTION

Often you need to execute more than one instruction after the THEN or the ELSE. In that case you may use the DO END sequence (see Figure 14.4 and 14.5). All the instructions between the DO and the END are performed one after another. Every DO must have its END. It is very important to indent properly so that you can match the DO's with their END's, so that the program is readable.

```
IF condition
   THEN
      DO
         instruction
         instruction
      END
```

Figure 14.4. DO END sequence.

```
IF A = B
THEN
   DO
      SAY "A is equal to B"
      A = B - 1
      SAY "but now it isn't"
   END
```

Figure 14.5. Example of an IF with a DO END sequence.

14.5 FUZZ: THE INEXACT COMPARISON

```
Normally,
123456789 <>  123456780      (not equal)


But:
NUMERIC FUZZ 1               (ignore one digit)
123456789  =  123456780      (are equal)


NUMERIC FUZZ 2               (ignore two digits)
123456789  =  123456722      (are equal)
```

Figure 14.6. Action of FUZZ.

Here's how FUZZ works. It tells REXX to ignore one or more digits in a comparison. It will ignore the least significant digit(s).

There are two things to think about here. First, is how many digits REXX is carrying in arithmetic operations, or the "NUMERIC DIGITS" setting. Normally this is nine. This means that REXX keeps track of nine significant digits. Another way to put it is that REXX's default precision is nine digits. The other thing to think about is FUZZ, or how many digits you want REXX to ignore in comparisons. NUMERIC FUZZ 1 says "out of the nine significant digits, ignore one low order digit".

In Figure 14.6, the default precision is nine. In the first comparison the two numbers are unequal, as they would be everywhere else on earth. In the second comparison, they are equal because NUMERIC FUZZ 1 told REXX to ignore the low order digit. In the third comparison NUMERIC FUZZ 2 tells REXX to ignore the two low order digits. This is a bit tricky. In Figure 14.7 the comparison is not equal, because there are not nine digits. There are only four. So, the FUZZ doesn't have a chance to work. However, in Figure 14.8, we said that there were five significant digits, and that REXX should ignore one. Since there actually are five significant digits the FUZZ works.

Notice Figure 14.9. This is like Figure 14.8, except that there are only four actual significant digits. So FUZZ doesn't work. Now look at Figure 14.10. We've told REXX that there are four significant digits, and there are four significant digits, so FUZZ works.

```
NUMERIC FUZZ 1
IF  2361 =  2362      /*is not equal*/
    THEN SAY "NOT YOUR NORMAL KIND OF MATH HERE"
    /* not equal because there
        aren't 9 significant digits*/
```

Figure 14.7. Example of FUZZ not giving equality.

```
NUMERIC DIGITS 5
NUMERIC FUZZ 1
IF 12361 = 12362      /*is equal*/
THEN SAY "NOT YOUR NORMAL KIND OF MATH HERE"
    /*equal because there are 5 significant digits*/
    /*FUZZ says ignore least significant digit*/
```

Figure 14.8. Example of FUZZ giving equality.

```
NUMERIC DIGITS 5
NUMERIC FUZZ 1
IF 02361 = 02362 /*not equal */
/* NOT EQUAL, because there are */
/* NOT 5 significant digits */
```

Figure 14.9. Example of FUZZ not giving equality.

```
NUMERIC DIGITS 4
NUMERIC FUZZ 1
IF 02361 = 02362       /*is equal*/
THEN SAY "NOT YOUR NORMAL KIND OF MATH HERE"
    /*equal because there are 4 significant digits*/
    /*FUZZ says ignore least significant digit*/
```

Figure 14.10. Example of FUZZ giving equality.

14.6 THE BOOLEAN OPERATORS


```
&         and
|         either or, or both
&&        only one is true. not both.
```

Figure 14.11. Boolean operators.

With Boolean operators you can do more that one comparison in an IF. You must use these operators, not the English words AND or OR (See Figure 14.11).

14.7 BOOLEAN EXAMPLES

```
IF TODAY = 'MONDAY' | TODAY = 'TUESDAY' |,
   TODAY = 'WEDNESDAY' | TODAY = 'THURSDAY' |,
   TODAY = 'FRIDAY'
   THEN SAY "HI HO! HI HO! OFF TO WORK I GO"

IF APPLICANT_A = 'WALKS ON WATER' &&,
   APPLICANT_A2 = 'CAN SWIM UNDER WATER 12 MINUTES"
   THEN SAY "YOU'RE HIRED      "
   ELSE SAY "SOUNDS FISHY TO ME"


IF DISH_CONTENTS_A = 'DILL PICKLES' &&,
   DISH_CONTENTS_B = 'CHOCOLATE MOUSSE"
   THEN SAY "YUMMY"
   ELSE SAY "YUCK "
```

Figure 14.12. Examples of Boolean operators.

14.8 HOW A COMPARISON BECOMES AN EXPRESSION

---

expression	is	becomes
"1" = "1"	True	1
"1" = "2"	False	0

Figure 14.13. Expressions are evaluated to 1 or 0.

When REXX evaluates an expression, the result of the evaluation is either a 1 or a 0. A 1 means "true", while a 0 means "false" (see Figure 14.13). Normally you don't see the 1 or the 0. REXX just uses the truth value to determine whether it should perform the instructions after the THEN or after the ELSE. What we're talking about here is the few instances when you actually see the result of the evaluation. There may be times when you want to make use of the 1 or the 0 in your program. Examine Figures 14.14 and 14.15 for some examples of this.

```
SAY "A" = "B"    /*says    0 */
SAY "A" = "A"    /*says    1 */

ANSWER = 32312.321 = 12193
SAY ANSWER       /*says    0*/
```

Figure 14.14. Examples of comparison expressions being evaluated to 1 or 0.

```
"ABC" = "CDE"    /*REXX will process it as follows:
                 "ABC" not a REXX keyword
                 not an assignment
                 not a command for TSO,
                 because of =.
                 So it's taken as a comparison
                 operation. IS "ABC" = "CDE" ?
                 Answer is no, which becomes 0.
                 REXX doesn't understand 0,
                 gives 0 to TSO.
                 TSO rejects it as invalid command */
```

Figure 14.15. Example that shows how REXX processes a comparison that is where an instruction should be.

14.9 QUESTIONS/PROBLEMS

Q 14.1: Is 43 = 4.3E1?

Q 14.2: Is 43 == 4.3E1?

Q 14.3: Complete this program segment:

```
/*REXX SAMPLE EXEC*/
NUMBER = 98765
IF NUMBER     12345
THEN

    SAY "THE NUMBER IS 12345"
    END
ELSE
    SAY "I DON'T KNOW WHAT IT IS EQUAL TO"
```

Problem 14.4: Write a program that will:
Store the number 12 as a constant
NUMBERA = 12
Store the number 13 as a constant
NUMBERB = 13
Then write the instructions that will compare the numbers and find them equal.

Q 14.5: What does this Exec display?
```
A = 5
B = 4
SAY A = B
```

Q 14.6: What does this Exec display?
```
A = 2 + 2 = 2
SAY A
```

Q 14.7: Which Boolean operator would you use here?
```
IF YANKEE_MANAGER_A = 'GREEN'          ,
YANKEE_MANAGER_B = 'DENT'
THEN SAY 'PLAY BALL'
```

Chapter 15

PARSING

This is an interesting chapter. It is about a capability of REXX that sets it apart from all other languages. A language that shines in the area of string manipulation can really allow you to write concise, streamlined programs. I believe that REXX excels in this area. I urge you to really study this chapter and try it out on your system, until you are completely comfortable with parsing in REXX.

Topics:

15.1 GENERAL FORM OF INSTRUCTION

```
PARSE [UPPER] origin template
```

origins   *templates*

    ARG   list of variables

    VAR   column delimiters

    PULL   literal delimiters

    SOURCE

    VALUE

    EXTERNAL

Figure 15.1. General form of the PARSE instruction.

In Figure 15.1 I show you a generalized form of the PARSE instruction. You start with the keyword PARSE. Next is an optional UPPER. If you specify UPPER, this instruction converts the data to upper case. If you don't specify it, the data is left as it was, upper, and lower mixed. Next is the origin. I give a list of the possible origins. These are different places that the data can come from. Note this important point: the instruction works the same way, regardless of the origin of the data. Finally, a template is used. The template acts as a filter on the data, influencing the way the data is placed in the destination variable(s). Another important point: Because an instruction like "PARSE UPPER ARG" is somewhat cumbersome, REXX allows you to abbreviate. You may say "ARG" instead of "PARSE UPPER ARG". In fact, you will rarely see "PARSE UPPER ARG" in any REXX program. The same goes for "PARSE UPPER PULL". You may abbreviate that as "PULL".

15.2 FUNCTION OF PARSING

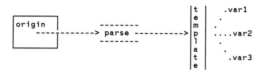

Figure 15.2. What PARSE does.

Figure 15.2 is a schematic of how PARSE works. PARSE takes data from one of several possible origins, passes it through a template and distributes the data into variables. All forms of PARSE work the same way, the only difference being the source of the data. Whenever you execute the PARSE instruction all the destination variables are changed. Some of the variables may receive the value "NULL", that is zero characters, but they are changed nevertheless. We will concentrate on the template very soon, but here I'd just like to say that the template may consist of:
1) just the variables (space is delimiter)
2) numbers designating columns (columns are delimiters)
3) literals (literals are delimiters).

15.3 THE ORIGINS

```
  origin of information                PARSE keyword

command line -------------------> ARG
variable -----------------------> VAR
the TSO stack ------------------> PULL
TSO info on how program
     was executed --------------> SOURCE
literal  -----------------------> VALUE
terminal -----------------------> EXTERNAL
```

Figure 15.3. Origins, where the information comes from on a PARSE.

Let's look at the different origins of the data that is PARSEd (see Figures 15.3 and 15.4).

1) the command line: when the program is executed (PARSE ARG, ARG). Parameters are passed to the program when it is executed, on the same line as the command that executes the program.

2) a variable (PARSE VAR): a variable may contain a string of characters consisting of any number of words, characters, spaces, or special characters. PARSE VAR allows you to break up that variable into several others.

3) the TSO STACK: an internal data queue that TSO maintains for the benefit of REXX programs (PARSE PULL).

4) information that TSO maintains about your REXX program. (PARSE SOURCE). You can use this to see whether you are under TSO or CMS.

5) a literal (PARSE VALUE): The data is specified in a literal. That may not seem very useful, but you may use a function instead of a literal. There will be an example of that later in this chapter. If you use this, you need the keyword WITH in order to tell where the literal ends.

6) the terminal (PARSE EXTERNAL): You can dialog with the terminal. I will give more details in the chapter on dialoguing with the terminal.

```
PARSE UPPER ARG VAR1 VAR2 VAR3
ARG VAR1 VAR2 VAR3 /* same as prev */

PARSE ARG VAR1 VAR2 VAR3

PARSE VAR NAME_AND_ADDRESS NAME ADDRESS

PARSE UPPER PULL REPLY_FROM_TERMINAL

PULL REPLY_FROM_TERMINAL

PARSE SOURCE  . . NAME OF EXEC ........ .

PARSE VALUE "TESTING ONE TWO" WITH VAR1 VAR2 VAR3

SAY "PLEASE ENTER YOUR NAME"
PARSE EXTERNAL NAME
PARSE UPPER EXTERNAL NAME /* same as prev */
```

Figure 15.4. Some examples of PARSE.

15.4 THE TEMPLATE WITH JUST VARIABLES

The template is essentially a list of variables. PARSE puts data in the variables. By using different types of templates you can gain more control over how information is put into the variables.

Figure 15.5 shows a PARSE ARG with only variables in the template. Let me remind you that the other forms of PARSE, PARSE PULL, PARSE VAR, etc, will work the same way. The information on the command line is placed in the variables shown in the instruction, with blanks delimiting what goes into each variable. One word goes into each variable, with a word being recognized by being surrounded by spaces. In this example there are just as many words as variables, so each word goes into a different variable, and each variable gets a word. The words are placed in the variables in the same order that they were entered. Please do not use commas here to delimit words. Spaces are used in a main program's ARG. In the chapter on Functions/Subroutines I'll show you when commas may be used on an ARG.

```
==>   %MYPRINT   MEMORIAL DRIVE     CAMBRIDGE



                   |        |         |
                   |        |         |
                   |        |         |
  /*REXX           V        V         V    PROGRM MYPRINT*/
  PARSE    ARG     LASTN    FIRSTN    ADDRESS
  SAY              FIRSTN   LASTN     ADDRESS
  /*DISPLAYS       DRIVE    MEMORIAL  CAMBRIDGE*/
```

Figure 15.5. Just variables in the template.

15.5 MORE VARIABLES THAN WORDS

If you have extra variables on the instruction, the extra variables contain nothing, they are made null. In Figure 15.6 FORTH contains nothing (null).

```
==>         %MYPRINT ONE     TWO     THREE

                     |       |       |     |
                     |       |       |     |
                     |       |       |     |
                     |       |       |     |
/*REXX     MYPRINT  V       V       V     V    EXEC  */
PARSE ARG           FRST    SECND   THIRD FORTH
SAY                 FRST    SECND   THIRD FORTH
/*DISPLAYS ONE TWO THREE         */
```

Figure 15.6. More variables than words.

15.6 MORE WORDS THAN VARIABLES

Let's see what happens when there are more words than variables that can receive them. REXX puts the extra words in the last variable. In Figure 15.7 there are three variables and four items of data. The last two are put in the third variable.

```
==>   %MYPRINT      ONE     TWO     3   4

                     |       |       |   |
                     |       |       |   |
                     |       |       |   |
/*REXX     MYPRINT  V       V       V   V    EXEC    */
PARSE     ARG       FRST    SECND   THIRD
SAY                 FRST    SECND   THIRD
/*DISPLAYS          ONE     TWO     3 4      */
```

Figure 15.7. More words than variables.

15.7 DROPPING EXTRA WORDS

If you know there are going to be extra items of information you can throw them away. If you use a period instead of a variable, the period absorbs the data that goes into it, and the data is thrown away. Use the period to ignore extra words, or items. There is an example of this in Figure 15.8. The period does not have to be last, so it can be used as a place holder.

```
==>      %MYPRINT ONE     TWO      3        4 5 6 7

                     |       |        |       | | | |
                     |       |        |       | | |_/
                     |       |        |       | |_/
                     |       |        |       |_/
/*REXX    MYPRINT V       V        V       V       */
PARSE     ARG     FRST    SECND THIRD    .
SAY       FRST    SECND THIRD
/*DISPLAYS ONE    TWO      3              */
```

Figure 15.8. Period absorbing extra words.

15.8 LITERAL IN A TEMPLATE

```
==> %RUNIT      HOW ARE YOU TODAY    (HOT ISN'T IT?
                 |   |   |   /        | |   |     /
                 |   |   |  /         | \   |    /
                 V   V   V/           V  \  V  /
        PARSE ARG ONE TWO THREE      "("    REST
```

Figure 15.9. Literal in a template.

If you use a literal character in a template it influences the way data is distributed into the variables. REXX will search for that literal character in the data. If it finds that character, it will put all the data that is before the character into the variables that are before the literal character. Then it will place all the data that is after the character into the variables that are after the literal character. In Figure 15.9, REXX will search for the left parenthesis. It will find it. Then it will split the data into two parts, the part before the parenthesis, and the part after the parenthesis. Then it splits the variables into two parts the same way. Then it distributes the data. Anything before the "(" goes into ONE, TWO and THREE. Anything after the "(" goes into REST. What is unique about this is that the "before", or left side has nothing to do with the "after", or right side. One side does not influence the other. It is as if there were two separate PARSE instructions.

Another way to look at it, is that the literal character forces a split of the data into two parts. An example of how this works is in Figure 15.10. You might be wondering what happens if the data does not contain the literal character. If that happens, the variables to the right of the literal character are set to null.

A very important thing to note is that the literal string may consist of one or more characters. This enables you to search for a specific word or sequence of characters.

```
/*ANOTHER REXX EXAMPLE  MYEXEC                        */
   PARSE UPPER ARG     QUESTION "?" ANSWER
   SAY "QUESTION" QUESTION
   SAY "ANSWER"   ANSWER

/*EXECUTED WITH ==> %MYEXEC WHAT'S MY NAME? TONY

/*DISPLAYS      QUESTION WHAT'S MY NAME      */
/*              ANSWER TONY                  */
```

Figure 15.10. Example of PARSE ARG with literal delimiter.

I have created a useful example of something you might do with this facility. Figure 15.11 illustrates how you can break up a dataset name into its component parts. A typical dataset name, with periods separating the parts of the name, and parentheses bracketing the member name, is put into a variable DSN. Then in the first PARSE it is broken into two pieces: *library* and *member*. Next, in the second PARSE, it is broken into three pieces where the periods are found.

```
/* REXX sample break up name */

DSN = "TRAIN01.ABC.COBOL(PROG1)"

PARSE VAR DSN LIBRARY "(" MEMBER ")"

PARSE VAR LIBRARY QUAL1 "." QUAL2 "." QUAL3 "." QUAL4

SAY "THE LIBRARY NAME WAS " LIBRARY
SAY "THE MEMBER NAME WAS  " MEMBER
SAY "QUALIFIER 1 " QUAL1
SAY "QUALIFIER 2 " QUAL2
SAY "QUALIFIER 3 " QUAL3
SAY "QUALIFIER 4 " QUAL4
```

Figure 15.11. Breaking up a typical dataset name using PARSE and literal strings.

15.9 VARIABLE INSTEAD OF A LITERAL

You may want to change the literal delimiter that you use. You can place the literal delimiter in a variable. However, you must enclose the variable in parentheses, so REXX will have a way of knowing that this particular variable contains a literal delimiter. Figure 15.12 will illustrate this. The variable SLSH could have contained any other literal delimiter.

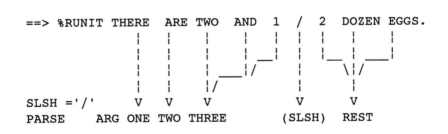

Figure 15.12. Using a Variable instead of a Literal.

15.10 COLUMN DELIMITING WITH SINGLE NUMBERS

Here is another way of delimiting the data. With this method you specify the columns that are to delimit the data. This allows you to use fixed format data, instead of variable format data as in the methods we showed you earlier in this chapter. When you use this method, spaces between words do not mean anything.

There is something tricky about this. The numbers don't mean exactly what they seem to. I suggest this easy way to figure out what columns go into a variable. To tell what columns go into a variable, look at the numbers on either side of it. The number on the left is the start column, the number on the right, minus 1, is the end column. That means that to figure out what happens in Figure 15.13, you would look at the numbers around VAR1. VAR1 is surrounded by 1 and 5. 1 is the number on the left, so that is the start column. 5 is the number on the right, so 5 minus 1 or 4 is the end column. Columns 1 through 4 go into VAR1. Similarly, VAR2 receives columns 5 through 8, and VAR3 receives columns 9 through 12.

```
==> %MYEXEC   ABCDEFGHIJKLMNOP

              ABCD          EFGH          IJKL
               |             |             |
               V             V             V
PARSE ARG 1 VAR1     5     VAR2     9     VAR3  13
```

Figure 15.13. Column delimiting with single numbers.

15.11 COLUMN DELIMITING WITH 2 NUMBERS

This is really not much different from the previous method, that used one number instead of two. This method allows you to skip columns, the previous method did not.

To determine which columns go into a variable, you do the same thing as in the previous method: you look at the numbers around it. The number on the left is the start column, and the number on the right, minus 1, is the end column. So in Figure 15.14, VAR1 is surrounded by 1 and 5, so VAR1 gets the data in columns 1 through 4. VAR2 is surrounded by 7 and 9, so VAR2 gets the data in columns 7 and 8. VAR3 is surrounded by 11 and 13, so

columns 11 and 12 go into VAR3.
Refer to Figure 15.15 for another example of delimiting with fixed columns.

```
==> %MYEXEC     ABCDEFGHIJKLMNOP

                ABCD        GH          KL
                 |          |           |
                 V          V           V
     PARSE ARG 1 VAR1 5   7 VAR2 9   11 VAR3 13
```

Figure 15.14. Column delimiting with two numbers.

```
==> %MYEXEC 1234567890ABCDEF

                   12           4            89
                    |           |            |
 /*REXX             |           |            |      */
                    V           V            V
     PARSE UPPER ARG 1 VAR1 3   4 VAR2 5   8 VAR3 10
     SAY               VAR1       VAR2        VAR3
```

Figure 15.15. Example of PARSE ARG with column delimiter.

15.12 PARSE VALUE

In Figure 15.16 you will see an example of PARSE VALUE with a literal, and with a function as well. REXX needs the keyword WITH so it can tell where the template begins. Using a literal doesn't seem to be very useful, but you may use a function instead of a literal. This figure uses the function TIME(). TIME() gives the time in the form: 12:01:22. We can make use of this by using literal delimiters with ":". REXX will split the time right at the colons, and place the hours into our variable HRS, the minutes into our variable MIN, and the seconds into our variable SEC.

```
PARSE VALUE "THIS IS A SAMPLE" WITH A B C D

PARSE VALUE TIME() WITH HRS ":" MIN ":" SEC
```

Figure 15.16. PARSE VALUE.

15.13 PARSE SOURCE

PARSE SOURCE asks TSO for information about the way the Exec was executed. There is an example of that in Figure 15.17. Notice that I had to continue the instruction on several lines with commas at the end of the first and second lines. Please note that PARSE SOURCE works differently on CMS. The CMS version has a different number of variables.

You may use the variable names I have used, or any others that are suitable. Figure 15.18 shows you what TSO may put in these variables when you execute the instruction.

```
PARSE SOURCE OP_SYSTEM HOW_CALLED EXEC_NAME,
    DD_NAME DATASET_NAME AS_CALLED
    DEFAULT_ADDRESS,
    NAME_OF_ADDRESS_SPACE
```

Figure 15.17. PARSE SOURCE on TSO.

OP_SYSTEM	TSO
HOW_CALLED	COMMAND, SUBROUTINE, or FUNCTION
EXEC_NAME	name of the Exec in uppercase.
DD_NAME	SYSEXEC or SYSPROC
DATASET_NAME	name of dataset the Exec was in. when called implicitly.
AS_CALLED	The name it was invoked by. ? when called implicitly. May be lower case
DEFAULT_ADDRESS	is the initial address environment generally TSO, MVS, ISPEXEC (for ISPF)
NAME_OF_ADDRESS_SPACE	TSO, MVS, or ISPF.

Figure 15.18. What goes into the variables on the PARSE SOURCE instruction.

5.14 QUESTIONS/PROBLEMS

Q 15.1: If you execute this Exec with the command shown
what are the results?
```
/*REXX RUNME    */
ARG YOUR_NAME ADDRESS        "/" JUNK
SAY "YOUR NAME IS " YOUR_NAME
SAY "YOU LIVE AT  " ADDRESS
.
= = > %RUNME JOHN 22 1/2 MAY ST LIMA PERU
```

Q 15.2: If you execute this Exec with the command shown
what are the results?
```
/*REXX RUNIT */
ARG  2 YOUR_NAME 5 6 ADDRESS 9
SAY "YOUR NAME IS " YOUR_NAME
SAY "YOU LIVE AT  " ADDRESS
= = > %RUNIT JOHN 22 1/2 MAY ST LIMA PERU
```

Problem 15.3: Write an Exec that accepts two ARGS:
Day of week, and Weather
If the weather is sunny or cloudy
and it's Friday,
display Head for Golf Course!
But if it's Friday and raining
display Head for Office!

Problem 15.4: Write an exec that breaks up the information
contained in a variable into three variables.
Place this information into the first variable VAR1:
ABCDEFGHIJKLMNOP
Use the proper PARSE instruction to break up the
first variable this way:
VAR2 gets columns 3 and 4
VAR3 gets columns 6 through 9
VAR4 gets columns 9 through 14
Display VAR2
Display VAR3
Display VAR4

Expected results:

CD
FGHI
IJKLMN

Chapter 16

ARG: PASSING INFORMATION TO THE PROGRAM

In this chapter I would like to explain what happens when you pass dataset names to your exec when you execute it, and give you some practice with the ARG/PARSE UPPER ARG instruction. As I pointed out in the preceding chapter, ARG is a short form of PARSE UPPER ARG. Be sure to create and test the execs described in the question/problem subsection.

Topics:

16.1 Passing Dataset Names
16.2 Questions/Problems

16.1 PASSING DATASET NAMES

One aspect of the ARG instruction that is worth mentioning is how the ARG handles dataset names. The rule here is simple: If the dataset name needs apostrophes, use them as in normal TSO commands. This means that when you execute a REXX exec, the way you handle dataset names is exactly the same as when you execute a normal TSO command. REXX does not change your habits! Examine Figures 16.1, 16.2 and 16.3 for examples of how this works.

```
/* REXX exec INFO: shows how to pass dataset names */
ARG DSN
"LISTDS " DSN
```

Figure 16.1. Sample exec. The next two figures illustrate executing it.

```
==> %INFO ABC.DATA
```

Figure 16.2. If the dataset name doesn't need apostrophes, don't use any.

```
==> %INFO   'SYS1.PROCLIB'
```

Figure 16.3. If the dataset name needs apostrophes, specify them.

16.2 QUESTIONS/PROBLEMS

Q 16.1: What would this say?
/*REXX EXEC testing */
ARG N1 N2 N3
SAY N2 N3 N1

If it is executed this way:
= = > %TESTING MARYELLEN SUE KAREN

Problem 16.2: Write an exec that will execute this TSO command:
LISTCAT ENTRY(dataset-name)
The dataset name is to be entered thru an ARG
Make sure it works on datasets belonging to you
as well as those belonging to someone else.

Try executing it with these two dataset names:
REXXPRGS.EXEC
'SYS1.PROCLIB'

= = > %myexec REXXPRGS.EXEC
= = > %myexec 'SYS1.PROCLIB'

Q 16.3: This ARG, and this manner of execution
produces what display?

/*REXX addemup exec */
ARG NUM1 NUM2 NUM3 .
TOTAL = NUM1 + NUM2 + NUM3
SAY TOTAL

= = = > %ADDEMUP 10 20 30 40 50 60

Problem 16.4: Write an Exec that accepts three pieces of
information and displays them in reverse order.
If more than 3 entered, display an error message
Expected results:
= = > %myexec peter paul mary
MARY PAUL PETER
= = > %myexec peter paul mary ringo
I said enter only three items please!

Problem 16.5: Write an Exec that examines information typed in
when it is executed
if both "Mike" and "George" are typed in, display
"incompatible attributes"
if only "Mike" typed in, display
"are you a Democrat?"
if only "George" typed in, display
"are you a Republican?"
if neither one is typed in, display an error message
Expected results:
= = = > %myexec mike george
INCOMPATIBLE ATTRIBUTES
= = = > %myexec mike
ARE YOU A DEMOCRAT?
= = = > %myexec george
ARE YOU A REPUBLICAN?
= = = > %myexec curly moe
PLEASE ENTER THE RIGHT NAMES

Chapter 17

DIALOGUING WITH THE TERMINAL

This chapter will detail how you can communicate with the person at the terminal, that is how you can accept information from the terminal and control prompting.

Topics:

17.1 FUNCTION OF PULL

PULL is the normal way of accepting information from the terminal (see Figure 17.1). There is only one thing wrong with that. As will be explained further in the chapter on the stack, PULL receives data from the stack as well as from the terminal. Sometimes this causes problems. Recall that PULL is a short form of PARSE UPPER PULL. Before you do a PULL from the terminal, you must always ask the person to type in the information. Otherwise, the keyboard unlocks, and the person at terminal won't know what to do.

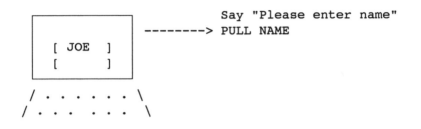

Figure 17.1. Function of the PULL instruction.

17.2 CAUTION REGARDING THE STACK

When you use the PULL instruction you must always be aware of what is in the stack. If there is anything in TSO's stack, PULL takes it from there and won't get what you type in at the terminal. One way of avoiding problems with that is shown in Figure 17.2.

```
/* Some things may be in the stack */
/* at this point.                  */
/* Newstack makes them inaccessible */
"NEWSTACK"
SAY "PLEASE ENTER NAME"
PULL NAME
/* Do says, pulls, pushes Execio here */
/* When finished, delete the stack */
"DELSTACK"
```

Figure 17.2. Example of a way of avoiding problems with anything that might be in the stack when you dialog with the terminal.

17.3 PARSE EXTERNAL-ANOTHER WAY

PARSE EXTERNAL takes information from the terminal, just as PULL does. (See Figure 17.3) You may use PARSE EXTERNAL as a way of bypassing the TSO stack.

If you use PARSE EXTERNAL you don't have to worry if anything is in the TSO stack. The only drawback of this is that you cannot execute this program from another one and pass to it, through the stack, the information it was going to request from the terminal. If that does not disturb you, feel free to use PARSE EXTERNAL. See Figure 17.4 for an example of the way that PARSE EXTERNAL bypasses the stack.

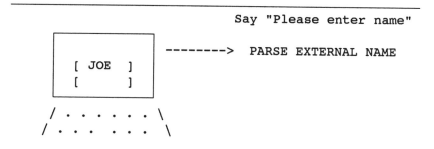

Figure 17.3. Another way of receiving information from the terminal.

```
Queue "this is in the stack"
Say "Please enter your name"
Parse External Name
Say "Thank you," Name
```

Figure 17.4. Example of PARSE EXTERNAL showing how the stack doesn't interfere with it.

17.4 TSO PROMPTING

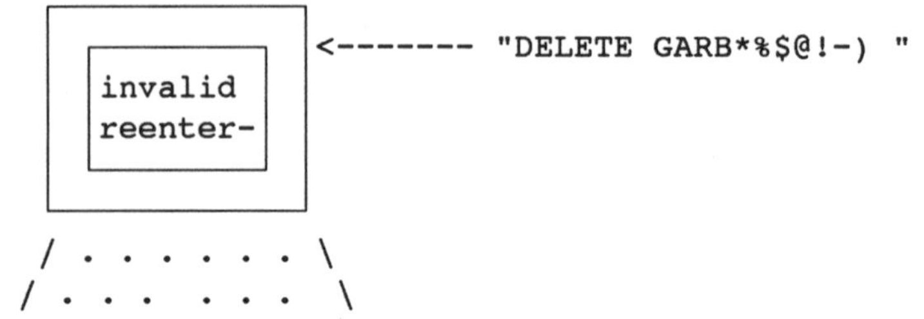

```
 _____
|  _____|    <------- "DELETE GARB*%$@!-) "
| |invalid|
| |reenter-|
| |_____|
|_____|
  / . . . . . . \
 / . . . .  . . \
```
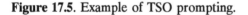

Figure 17.5. Example of TSO prompting.

TSO's prompting uses the same stack as PUSHES and PULLS. This means that you may stack information that a prompt will ask for. Before you allow any TSO command to prompt you in a REXX exec, you must know that prompting in a REXX exec defaults to OFF, while prompting outside of an exec, in TSO, defaults to ON.

If you wish to allow a TSO command to do any prompting in your REXX exec, you must first execute the TSO command "PROFILE PROMPT", then you must turn it on for the exec. Turn it on for the exec with the PROMPT function. Figure 17.6 shows how to turn on prompting and save the previous setting. Figure 17.7 shows how to restore the previous setting. Figure 17.8 shows how you can display the current setting. Figure 17.9 is a fuller example of how you can allow prompting. Note that pressing PA1 or ATTN will cancel the prompt and your program as well.

```
    "PROFILE PROMPT"
    SAVE_PROMPT = PROMPT('ON')
```

Figure 17.6. How to turn on prompting and save previous setting.

```
DUMMY = PROMPT(SAVE_PROMPT)
```

Figure 17.7. How to restore the previous setting.

```
SAY PROMPT()
```

Figure 17.8. Displaying the current setting of PROMPT.

```
/* REXX exec that shows how a command
may be allowed to prompt */
"PROFILE PROMPT"
X = PROMPT("ON")
"NEWSTACK"
/* Commands that prompt here   */
"DELETE ABC*&^%$.d()+#"
"DELSTACK"
```

Figure 17.9. Example of how you can allow a command to prompt.

17.5 QUESTIONS/PROBLEMS

Q 17.1: You want the user to type in 3 and only 3 items
(words) of information, separated by spaces.
What does your PULL look like?

Problem 17.2: Write an Exec that asks for 3 words (only)
and displays them in reverse order.
Expected results:
= = = > %myexec a b c
C B A
= = = > %myexec a b c d
C B A

Problem 17.3: Write a front end exec for the DELETE command.
Have it ask "are you sure?"
If the data set name is "junk.data" don't ask.

Expected results:
= = = > %erase abc.data
ARE YOU SURE? Y/N
= = = > n
NOT DELETED
= = = > %erase junk.data
DELETED

Problem 17.4: Write an Exec that computes the percent of increase
of one number over another
Ask for the two amounts from the terminal

The formula is:
% increase =   100 * ((new - old) / old)

Imagine your old salary was 21,203
and your new is 80,000

You would figure the % increase as
% increase =   100 * ((80000 - 21203) / 21203)

Expected results:
= = = > %myexec 100 120
20

Problem 17.5: Ask for the weather from the terminal,
and the day of the week.
If it's raining, ask how many inches
If it's Friday and sunny, or cloudy
display "head for golf course"
If it's Saturday and less than .5 inches,
display "fishing pole please"

Expected results:
= = = > %myexec
WHAT DAY OF THE WEEK?
= = = > FRIDAY
WHAT IS THE WEATHER?
= = = > SUNNY
HEAD FOR GOLF COURSE
= = = > %myexec
WHAT DAY OF THE WEEK?
= = = > SATURDAY
WHAT IS THE WEATHER?
= = = > RAINING
HOW MANY INCHES?
.4
FISHING POLE PLEASE

Chapter 18

DEBUGGING

In this chapter I will show you the TSO commands that affect debugging and interactive trace. I will show you how to stop your program during execution, and to turn on debugging. I will explain what you can do during interactive debugging, and point out the instructions that you can place in your exec that control debugging.

Topics:

18.1 What you can do in TSO before Executing
18.2 What you can do in TSO during Execution
18.3 What you put in the Exec
18.4 Keyword TRACE
18.5 EXECUTIL in the Exec
18.6 During Interactive Debug
18.7 Codes Displayed during Interactive Debug
18.8 Questions/Problems

18.1 WHAT YOU CAN DO IN TSO BEFORE EXECUTING

Figure 18.1 tells you how to turn on interactive debugging before executing your exec. Type in the TSO command EXECUTIL TS. This will turn on interactive debugging for the next REXX exec that you run. If you want interactive debugging for the one after that, you'll have to turn it on again.

```
EXECUTIL TS
```

Figure 18.1. Turning on interactive debugging for the next exec that you run.

18.2 WHAT YOU CAN DO IN TSO, DURING EXECUTION

While your exec is executing, there are several things you can do to affect its execution. If you press PA1, or on some systems, the ATTN key, you will interrupt the execution of your exec. Refer to Figure 18.2. You will see that after you press PA1 or ATTN, you can stop your exec and put it into interactive debug by typing in TS. You can just stop the exec and return to TSO by typing in HI. HT will cancel the output of a SAY or a TRACE. TE will stop all tracing. You generally use this when your exec is running with some kind of tracing turned on, but not interactive debug. This will stop the tracing. If you press ENTER, your exec will continue as if you hadn't interrupted it. Figure 18.3 illustrates the message that TSO displays after you press PA1 or ATTN during your program's execution.

```
        PA1 or ATTN, then

         HI    Halt Interpret
         TS    Trace Start
         HT    Halt Typing
         RT    Resume Typing
         TE    Trace End
     (ENTER) Continue
```

Figure 18.2. Controlling the execution of your exec.

```
    (After pressing PA1 or ATTN)

ENTER HI  TO END,  A  NULL  LINE  TO  CONTINUE,  OR  AN
IMMEDIATE COMMAND

         HI
         TS
         HT
         RT
         TE
```

Figure 18.3. Message displayed when you interrupt the execution of your program.

18.3 WHAT YOU PUT IN THE EXEC

Figure 18.4 shows you some instructions you may place in the exec that affect debugging. You will most likely remove these instructions when your exec is placed into production. You should note that the main part of your program and its subroutines do not share tracing settings. The subroutines do inherit trace settings from the main part of the program, but any change made to trace settings inside of a subroutine does not affect the main part of the program. This means that you may place these instructions in a subroutine to control just the subroutine.

```
TRACE    [!]type-of-tracing
TRACE    [?]type-of-tracing

          type-of-tracing:
            N       (Normal)
            E       (Error)
            F       (Failure)
            C       (Commands)
            A       (All)
            R       (Results)
            I       (Intermediate)
            L       (Labels)
            S       (Scan)
            O       (Off)

"EXECUTIL TS "
"EXECUTIL TE "
"EXECUTIL HT "
"EXECUTIL RT "
```

Figure 18.4. Debugging instructions you may put in the exec.

18.4 KEYWORD TRACE

The TRACE instruction may take two forms in your exec. First, it may appear in the form TRACE type-of-tracing, for example TRACE I. It may also appear as TRACE ?type-of-tracing, for example TRACE ?I or TRACE !type-of-tracing, for example TRACE !I. See Figure 18.5 for an explanation of the meaning of the ? and the !.

When you use type-of-tracing, you just specify the first letter of the option, as for example TRACE I, meaning TRACE Intermediate. See Figure 18.6 for a list of the types of tracing available, and their meanings. Figure 18.7 shows you some examples of TRACE with and without ? and !.

```
!  means Don't execute any commands meant for TSO, ISPF
         I.E. Ignore any environment commands.
         Useful if the command could have serious
         consequences.

!  done again, sets that option off, so commands ARE executed
         (it toggles)

?  means Turn on Interactive debug

?  done again, turns off interactive debug (it toggles)
```

Figure 18.5. Meaning of ? and ! on the TRACE instruction.

```
TRACE Normal          default. just show commands to
                      environment that fail with negative
                      return code

TRACE Error           just show commands to environment
                      that fail with non-zero return code

TRACE Failure         just show commands to environment
                      that are not found

TRACE Commands        show commands to environment

TRACE All             show all clauses

TRACE Results         show all clauses and final result
                      just before execution. Good choice.

TRACE Intermediate    show all clauses, intermediate or
                      partial results, and final result.

TRACE Labels          just show labels entered

TRACE Scan            just show clauses, don't execute them

TRACE Off             no more tracing of any kind.
```

Figure 18.6. Meanings of type-of-trace.

```
TRACE ?A       /* turn on interactive trace*/
               /* and trace everything*/

TRACE ?L       /* turn on interactive trace*/
               /* and trace labels*/

TRACE !C       /* don't execute TSO commands*/
               /* but trace  them       */

TRACE !N       /* don't execute TSO commands*/
               /* trace only if some error */

TRACE  L       /* trace labels           */


TRACE  I       /* trace intermediate results */
```

Figure 18.7. Examples of TRACE.

18.5 EXECUTIL IN THE EXEC

You may use the EXECUTIL TSO command in the exec to control tracing.
See Figure 18.8 for an explanation of the options of EXECUTIL.

```
"EXECUTIL TS"    turns on interactive debug

"EXECUTIL TE"    turns off interactive debug

"EXECUTIL HT"    stops displays to terminal

"EXECUTIL RT"    resumes displays to terminal
```

Figure 18.8. Options of EXECUTIL.

18.6 DURING INTERACTIVE DEBUG

Interactive debug in REXX is truly amazing. Although your program is stopped, you can interact with it. You can view and change your program's variables, and execute any instruction that would be legal inside the exec. The only thing you may not do is change your program's statements. That will have to wait until you finish with interactive debug. Figure 18.9 lists some of the things you can do during interactive debug.

When your program is in interactive debug, it stops after executing each instruction. You can execute one instruction at a time by just pressing ENTER. That way you can watch what happens as it executes. Interactive debug gives you an automatic TRACE R. You can re-execute the last instruction that just executed, by typing in "=". This is useful when you have just changed a variable and want to reexecute an instruction to see how it works this time. You may display and change variables, issue commands to TSO, type EXIT to end the exec, type LOGOFF to sign off from TSO.

A very useful function is the one which displays the actual line of your program as you wrote it: SAY SOURCELINE(number). You could even type this in, on one line, to display the complete program:
DO I = 1 TO 9999;SAY SOURCELINE(I);END

```
(ENTER)              single step execution
=                    reexecute last command
"EXECUTIL TE"        stop tracing
 TRACE [!] type-of-tracing
 TRACE [?] type-of-tracing

.TRACE OFF           stop tracing
 Any instruction

 Any command

 Display variables

 Change variables
```

Figure 18.9. What you can do during interactive debug.

18.7 CODES DISPLAYED DURING INTERACTIVE DEBUG

While your program is executing in interactive debug, REXX will display certain codes to tell you just what the display means. Figure 18.10 lists those codes.

```
*-* original program line

+++ trace message

>>> result of an expression.   During TRACE R

>.> value assigned to a placeholder (period)
    during Parsing.

>C> The resolved name of a compound variable

>F> result of a function call

>L> a literal

>O> result of an operation on two terms

>P> result of a prefix operation

>V> contents of a variable.
```

Figure 18.10. Codes displayed during TRACE.

18.8 QUESTIONS/PROBLEMS

Q 18.1: Your program is running, apparently not doing anything, and won't stop. What do you type in to see what it is doing?

Q 18.2: You are in interactive trace, single stepping through the program. You've had enough. What do you type in to make the program run without any trace?

Q 18.3: Can you regain control of your runaway Exec by
typing in "EXECUTIL TS " ?

Q 18.4: Can you put "EXECUTIL TS" in your Exec
to turn on interactive debug?

Chapter 19

TRAPPING ERRORS

This chapter will show you how to intercept error conditions that may occur during your program's execution. It will show you how to set up condition traps in your programs to trap syntax errors, command failures, undefined variables, and an interrupt. Last, it will show you how an unconditional transfer of control is done.

Topics:

19.1 FUNCTION OF THE TRAP

REXX allows you to set up a routine in your program to trap five exceptional conditions. If these conditions occur, control jumps to the routine you have set up. You can take some action at that point, and most likely terminate the program.
 The routine is physically located at the end of your program. Control must not fall into the trap, so you must place an EXIT just before the first trap routine. In order to activate the trap, you must include a statement near the beginning of your program that initializes the trap.

19.2 GENERAL APPEARANCE OF THE TRAP

The most common type of trap is the one that terminates your program. It is physically near the end of your program, begins with a label and ends with the word EXIT. Near the beginning of your program you will have a statement that turns on the trap, with the SIGNAL ON instruction.

Figure 19.1 shows the general form of the trap that terminates. Another type of trap you may use is the type that continues after the error condition is detected. The trap is physically located at the end of your program. It begins with a label, and ends with a RETURN. The RETURN may not pass back any information. This is actually a subroutine call. Near the beginning of the program you must place the statement that initializes the trap, with the CALL ON instruction. Figure 19.2 illustrates the general form of the trap that continues.

Normally, as you will see in the forthcoming examples, the trap is named the same as the error condition you want to trap. You may name the trap that continues anything you want, however. Figure 19.3 shows you the general form of the trap that continues, named anything you want.

```
SIGNAL ON condition
       .
       .

EXIT
condition:
/* handle condition */
       .
       .

EXIT
```

Figure 19.1. General form of the trap that terminates.

```
CALL    ON condition
        .

        .

EXIT
condition:
/* handle condition */
        .


        .
RETURN ""
```

Figure 19.2. General form of the trap that continues.

```
CALL    ON condition,
        NAME routine-name
        .


        .
EXIT
routine-name:
/* handle condition */
        .


        .
RETURN ""
```

Figure 19.3. General form of the trap that continues, named any way you want.

19.3 TRAPPING SYNTAX ERROR

You may trap REXX syntax errors. This will intercept the situation where REXX cannot interpret your instruction. Figure 19.4 contains examples of the type of error that the syntax trap will catch.

If you don't have a syntax trap, REXX displays the line in error, displays an error message, and stops your program. Figure 19.5 is an example of a syntax error trap that terminates. Figure 19.6 is an example of a syntax error trap that continues, changing the name of the trap to OOPS. To turn off the trap, use SIGNAL OFF SYNTAX.

```
Say "A" - "B"
X = (Cur - Prev / Prev
```

Figure 19.4. Examples of syntax error.

```
SIGNAL ON SYNTAX

SAY "A" - "B"

.

.

EXIT
SYNTAX:
 SAY "SYNTAX ERROR"
/* display other messages.
    see figure 19.19 */
EXIT
```

Figure 19.5. Example of a syntax error trap that terminates

```
CALL    ON SYNTAX,
        NAME OOPS
SAY "A" - "B"
  .


  .
EXIT
OOPS:
 SAY "SYNTAX ERROR"
/* display other messages.
   see figure 19.19 */
RETURN ""
```

Figure 19.6. Example of a syntax error trap that continues.

19.4 TRAPPING ERROR

The ERROR trap intercepts the failure of known TSO and ISPF commands. The return code of the command was greater than zero. The command was legitimate, but was unable to complete, for example trying to delete a dataset that doesn't exist. Figure 19.7 shows examples of what ERROR traps. If you have no FAILURE trap, ERROR traps that too.

If you don't have an error trap, REXX displays the command that failed and continues with the Exec. You should note that some commands give a return code greater than zero, when they work, and send to the trap. "MAKEBUF" is a TSO command that would always send to the trap. Figure 19.8 is an example of an ERROR trap that terminates. Figure 19.9 is an example of an ERROR trap that continues, and uses the name BADTSOCMD for the subroutine. To turn off the trap use SIGNAL OFF ERROR.

```
"LISTALC JUNK"
"DELETE NONE.SUCH"
```

Figure 19.7. Examples of what ERROR traps.

```
SIGNAL ON ERROR
"LISTALC JUNK"
        .


        .
EXIT
ERROR:
 SAY "COMMAND FAILED"
/* display other messages.
   see figure 19.19 */
 EXIT
```

Figure 19.8. Example of ERROR trap that terminates.

```
CALL   ON ERROR NAME BADTSOCMD
"LISTALC JUNK"
        .


        .
EXIT
BADTSOCMD:
 SAY "COMMAND FAILED"
/* display other messages.
   see figure 19.19 */
RETURN ""
```

Figure 19.9. Example of ERROR trap that continues.

19.5 TRAPPING FAILURE

The FAILURE trap intercepts the severe failure of commands to the environment. This situation arises when the command does not exist, (TSO gives a minus 3 return code in RC), the command or program abends, is aborted by TSO which assigns an abend code. The abend code is converted to a decimal number which appears in RC. If it was a System abend code the number is negative. If it was a User abend code the number is positive. To convert the code back to the original form, use SAY C2X(ABS(RC)). This will convert unfamiliar abend codes to familiar ones, such as 0C7 and 013. Figure 19.10 shows examples of what FAILURE can intercept. If you don't have a FAILURE trap, REXX displays the command that failed and continues with the Exec. To turn off the trap, use SIGNAL OFF FAILURE. Figure 19.11 is an example of a FAILURE trap that terminates. Figure 19.12 is an example of a FAILURE trap that continues, and changes the name of the subroutine to CMDFAIL.

```
"THIS IS NOT A TSO CMD"
"LISTDOG"
"CALL 'BADLUCK.LIB(BOOM)'"
```

Figure 19.10. Example of what FAILURE traps.

```
SIGNAL ON FAILURE
"THIS IS NOT A TSO CMD"
"LISTDOG"
"CALL 'BADLUCK.LIB(BOOM)'"
        .

        .

EXIT
FAILURE:
 SAY "COMMAND FAILED. CODE " C2X(ABS(RC))
/* display other messages.
    see figure 19.19 */
 EXIT
```

Figure 19.11. Example of a FAILURE trap that terminates.

```
CALL ON FAILURE,
          NAME CMDFAIL
"THIS IS NOT A TSO CMD"
"LISTDOG"
"CALL 'BADLUCK.LIB(BOOM)'"
          .

          .

EXIT
CMDFAIL:
 SAY "COMMAND FAILED"
 SAY "CODE IS " C2X(ABS(RC))
 /* display other messages.
    see figure 19.19 */
 RETURN ""
```

Figure 19.12. Example of a FAILURE trap that continues.

19.6 TRAPPING NOVALUE

It is legal to use a variable that was never given a value, REXX just takes it as a literal, but you can trap that, however. This can be useful in debugging, but after your program is thoroughly tested, there is generally no need to leave in a NOVALUE trap. Figure 19.13 contains examples of uninitialized variables being used. If you don't set up a novalue trap, undefined variables are taken as literals and the exec continues without interruption. To turn off the NOVALUE trap, use SIGNAL OFF NOVALUE. Figure 19.14 is an example of a NOVALUE trap that terminates. Figure 19.15 is an example of a NOVALUE trap that continues, and changes the name of its subroutine to PLEASE_INIT.

```
/* REXX Exec */
SAY HELLO
X = Y + 1
```

Figure 19.13. Example of what NOVALUE traps.

```
SIGNAL ON NOVALUE
SAY HELLO
        .


        .

EXIT
NOVALUE:
 SAY "PLEASE DEFINE YOUR VARIABLES"
/* display other messages.
   see figure 19.19 */
EXIT
```

Figure 19.14. Example of NOVALUE trap that terminates.

```
CALL ON NOVALUE NAME PLEASE_INIT
SAY HELLO
        .


        .

EXIT
PLEASE_INIT:
 SAY "PLEASE DEFINE YOUR VARIABLES"
/* display other messages.
   see figure 19.19 */
RETURN ""
```

Figure 19.15. Example of NOVALUE trap that continues.

19.7 TRAPPING PA1/ATTN

You may trap the user interrupting with PA1 or ATTN (see Figure 19.16).

If you don't set up a HALT trap, the program will be stopped when the PA1 or ATTN key is pressed, and HI is typed in. I recommend that you not prevent the user from stopping the execution of the program. Figure 19.17 is an example of a HALT trap that terminates. Figure 19.18 is an example of a HALT trap that continues, and changes the name of its subroutine to BYE. To turn off the HALT trap, use SIGNAL OFF HALT.

Figure 19.16. Effect of trapping interrupts.

```
SIGNAL ON HALT
        .


        .

EXIT
HALT:
 SAY "DON'T INTERRUPT"
/* display other messages.
    see figure 19.19 */
EXIT
```

Figure 19.17. Example of a HALT trap that terminates.

```
CALL ON HALT NAME BYE



BYE:
 SAY "WANT TO STOP? Y/N"
PULL REPLY
IF REPLY = "Y" THEN EXIT
RETURN ""
```

Figure 19.18. Example of a HALT trap that gives a choice about terminating.

19.8 WHAT YOU CAN PUT IN THE TRAP

You may put any REXX instruction or TSO command in your trap, but there are certain things that are particularly useful. Figure 19.19 illustrates several of these.

The special REXX variable SIGL contains the line number of the statement that sent you to the error trap. The function SOURCELINE(line number) gives the actual program statement that you wrote in the program. The function ERRORTEXT(RC) gives the message that REXX would normally display for the REXX error. The function CONDITION("D") displays the string in error. This can be useful in pinpointing the exact cause of the error.

```
label:
SAY "ERROR ON LINE " SIGL
SAY "LINE CONTAINING ERROR IS "    SOURCELINE(SIGL)
SAY "THE PROBLEM IS IN:"          CONDITION("D")
SAY "ERROR MESSAGE FROM REXX IS " ERRORTEXT(RC)
EXIT
```

Figure 19.19. Examples of what you can put in the trap.

19.9 EXAMPLES

```
/*REXX sample showing condition traps*/
SIGNAL ON ERROR
SIGNAL ON SYNTAX
SIGNAL ON FAILURE
SIGNAL ON NOVALUE
"DELETE NO.SUCH.DATASET"
"WHAT COMMAND IS THIS  "
SALARY-INCREASE = 10
SAY ERROR_MESSAGE
EXIT
ERROR:
SAY "COMMAND TO TSO DID NOT WORK"
SAY "ON LINE " SIGL
SAY "COMMAND WAS " SOURCELINE(SIGL)
EXIT

FAILURE:
SAY "COMMAND TO TSO DID NOT WORK"
SAY "ON LINE " SIGL
SAY "COMMAND WAS " SOURCELINE(SIGL)
SAY "ABEND CODE: " C2X(ABS(RC))
IF RC = -3 THEN SAY "COMMAND NOT FOUND"
EXIT

SYNTAX:
SAY "SYNTAX ERROR IN PROGRAM"
SAY "ON LINE " SIGL
SAY "INSTRUCTION WAS " SOURCELINE(SIGL)
SAY "REXX ERROR MSG: " ERRORTEXT(RC)
SAY "PROBLEM IS IN:"  CONDITION("D")
EXIT

NOVALUE:
SAY "UNDEFINED VARIABLE      "
SAY "ON LINE " SIGL
SAY "THE VARIABLE IS:" CONDITION("D")
SAY "INSTRUCTION WAS " SOURCELINE(SIGL)
EXIT
```

Figure 19.20. Examples of condition traps that terminate.

```
/*REXX sample showing condition traps*/
CALL   ON ERROR
SIGNAL ON SYNTAX
SIGNAL ON FAILURE
CALL ON   NOVALUE  NAME NOINIT
"DELETE NO.SUCH.DATASET"
"WHAT COMMAND IS THIS  "
SALARY-INCREASE = 10
SAY ERROR_MESSAGE


EXIT

ERROR:
SAY "COMMAND TO TSO DID NOT WORK"
SAY "ON LINE " SIGL
SAY "COMMAND WAS " SOURCELINE(SIGL)
RETURN

FAILURE:
SAY "COMMAND TO TSO DID NOT WORK"
SAY "ON LINE " SIGL
SAY "COMMAND WAS " SOURCELINE(SIGL)
SAY "ABEND CODE: " RC
IF RC = -3 THEN SAY "COMMAND NOT FOUND"
EXIT

SYNTAX:
SAY "SYNTAX ERROR IN PROGRAM"
SAY "ON LINE " SIGL
SAY "INSTRUCTION WAS " SOURCELINE(SIGL)
SAY "REXX ERROR MSG: " ERRORTEXT(RC)
SAY "PROBLEM IS IN:"   CONDITION("D")
EXIT
NOINIT:
SAY "UNDEFINED VARIABLE      "
SAY "ON LINE " SIGL
SAY "THE VARIABLE IS:" CONDITION("D")
SAY "INSTRUCTION WAS " SOURCELINE(SIGL)
RETURN
```

Figure 19.21. Examples of condition traps that terminate and that continue.

19.10 THE INFAMOUS "GO TO"

There is a form of the SIGNAL instruction that acts like a GO TO. The SIGNAL instruction can send to a label, even without any error. This is the unconditional transfer of control, or GO TO. It should not be used like a GO TO in traditional programming languages. It is not needed in REXX, since REXX is so completely endowed with structured programming constructs, that you may handle all logic situations in REXX without using SIGNAL as a GO TO. If you do it, I suggest you EXIT in the routine. Signal should not be used to get out of a loop, because it destroys loop control structures, and REXX provides an orderly way of exiting from a loop. (LEAVE)

```
               SIGNAL THE_END
                     .
                     .


               THE_END:
                     .
                     .

               EXIT
```

Figure 19.22. Using SIGNAL like a GO TO.

19.11 QUESTIONS/PROBLEMS

Q 19.1: Should you leave ERROR traps in Execs that go into production?

Q 19.2: Does the NOVALUE trap help to enforce a good programming practice?

Q 19.3: ERRORTEXT(RC) is used in which error trap?

Q 19.4: Complete this Exec
        /*REXX sample exec*/
        SIGNAL ON ERROR
        SIGNAL ON
        "TURN DOWN VOLUME"
        SAY 1 * (2 + 3 (
        EXIT

        SAY "COMMAND TO TSO FAILED"

        SYNTAX:
        SAY "SYNTAX ERROR ON LINE "
        EXIT

Problem 19.5: Write an Exec that asks for a dataset name and then issues the
TSO command LISTD on it. Set up an error trap to intercept the command
not working. In the error trap, display the line of the program in error, the
error code from TSO. Ask for the dataset name again, reexecute the
command and exit.

        Expected results:
        = = = > %myexec
            PLEASE ENTER DATASET NAME
        = = = > abc.nonesuch.data
            CANNOT EXECUTE TSO COMMAND
            TSO ERROR CODE IS 12
            LINE IN ERROR IS LISTDS dsn
            PLEASE REENTER
        = = = > abc.real.data
            ABC.REAL.DATA VOLUME SERIAL D12345
            LRECL 80 BLKSIZE 3120 RECFM FB

Chapter 20

MATH

This chapter will concentrate on the way REXX does arithmetic. You will see how to use REXX's arithmetic operators, and to change the precision for arithmetic operations.

Topics:

20.1 WHEN IS MATH DONE?

```
A = 1 + 1

SAY 1 + 1
```

Figure 20.1. Examples of when math is done.

REXX will do math anytime it finds arithmetic operators and two or more numbers that are not inside of quotes or apostrophes. REXX does math especially on the SAY instruction, and in the assignment statement. Figure 20.1 illustrates an assignment statement, and a Say instruction.

125

Please note that you must use the operators in REXX, and that you may not use words. The operators in REXX are like those in most other languages, except that REXX uses "%" for integer division, and "//" for the remainder of a division.

Finally, I'd like to point out that REXX will do the logical evaluation of expressions such as in "SAY 1 = 2", but that this is not math.

20.2 OPERATORS

+	add
-	subtract
*	multiply
/	divide
%	integer divide
//	give remainder of division
**	raise to a power. (whole numbers only) negative exponents work
-	prefix on a number. (-1) take it as negative
+	prefix on a number. (+1) take it as positive
( )	to group items

Figure 20.2. Arithmetic operators in REXX.

```
1  + 1   = 2

2  - 1   = 1

2  * 2   = 4

4  / 2   = 2

5  % 2   = 2

5 // 2   = 1

3 ** 2   = 9

-1 * 2   = -2

(4 + 2) * 3    = 18
```

Figure 20.3. Examples of the arithmetic operators.

20.3 PRECISION

REXX can do math to any precision. The only limitation is the amount of memory that is available on your system. A precision of 10,000 seems to work on most systems. REXX is amazingly fast, in spite of the large number of digits being carried in arithmetic operations. Recall that the default is 9. Figure 20.4 illustrates REXX performing a division to 100 digits. Rounding will take place when there are more digits than the precision allows. For example, 1234567809 will be changed to 1234567810, and displayed as 1.23456781E+9.

You may want to refer back to the chapter on the IF for information on FUZZ allowing approximation in comparisons.

```
SAY    2 / 3

/*displays    .666666667
              (9 digits)    */

NUMERIC DIGITS    100

SAY 2 / 3

/*displays
.666666666666666666666666666666666666666
666666666666666666666666666666666666666
6666666666666666667    */
```

Figure 20.4. Example of REXX doing math to 100 digits of precision.

20.4   CONTROLLING HOW LARGE NUMBERS ARE DISPLAYED

You may control the manner is which large numbers are displayed with the NUMERIC FORM instruction. NUMERIC FORM SCIENTIFIC would give a number in the form: 1.23E+13. NUMERIC FORM ENGINEERING would give a number in the form: 12.3E+12.

20.5 QUESTIONS/PROBLEMS

Problem 20.1: Write an Exec that will multiply two numbers,
   prompt the user for the two numbers,
   set up an error trap to intercept any error,
   such as invalid numbers.

Problem 20.2: Run this Exec to determine the effect of
   parentheses on arithmetic operations.

   SAY (1 + 2) * 3
   SAY 1 + (2 * 3)
   SAY 1 + 2 * 3
   What is displayed?

Problem 20.3: Write an Exec that asks for a number (record length)
   and another number (block size).
   It determines if block size is an exact multiple
   of record length, I.E. if record length was
   multiplied by a whole number to obtain block size.
   Expected results:
   = = = > %myexec
      PLEASE ENTER RECORD LENGTH
   = = = > 80
      PLEASE ENTER BLOCK SIZE
   = = = > 3121
      BLOCK SIZE IS NOT A MULTIPLE OF RECORD LENGTH

Chapter 21

SELECT: THE CASE STRUCTURE

This chapter is about the REXX implementation of the Case structure. You will see how to choose among several possible alternative actions with SELECT.

Topics:

21.1 Function of the SELECT
21.2 Syntax of the SELECT
21.3 Questions/Problems

21.1 FUNCTION OF THE SELECT

SELECT is REXX's implementation of the structured programming construct CASE. SELECT tests a series of conditions, one after the other. As soon as it finds a true condition, it executes the instruction associated with that condition, and exits from the structure. If none of the conditions are true, the OTHERWISE instruction is executed.

21.2 SYNTAX OF THE SELECT

I suggest you place the SELECT, the WHENs, the OTHERWISE, and the END all on separate lines as shown in Figure 21.1. Each WHEN introduces an expression, that is a comparison that will be tested in turn by the instruction. Each WHEN must have a THEN that introduces an instruction that is to be executed if its condition is true. There may be only one instruction after the THEN, but you may use several instructions if you place them between a DO and an END, just as with the IF. There may be as many WHENs as desired.

The OTHERWISE is required, and introduces one instruction, or several instructions if they are between a DO and an END. Figure 21.2 shows an example of the SELECT.

```
SELECT
    WHEN    expression-1 THEN    instruction-1
    WHEN    expression-2 THEN    instruction-2
    WHEN    expression-3 THEN    instruction-3
    WHEN    expression-4 THEN    instruction-4
    WHEN    expression-5 THEN    instruction-5
    WHEN    expression-6 THEN    instruction-6
    . . .
    WHEN    expression-n THEN    instruction-n
    OTHERWISE    instruction-x
    END
```

Figure 21.1. Syntax of the SELECT.

```
SELECT
    WHEN    DAY = 1      THEN    SAY "SUNDAY"
    WHEN    DAY = 2      THEN    SAY "MONDAY"
    WHEN    DAY = 3      THEN    SAY "TUESDAY"
    WHEN    DAY = 4      THEN    SAY "WEDNESDAY"
    WHEN    DAY = 5      THEN    SAY "THURSDAY"
    WHEN    DAY = 6      THEN    SAY "FRIDAY"
    WHEN    DAY = 7      THEN    SAY "SATURDAY"
    OTHERWISE    SAY "UNKNOWN DAY"
    END
```

Figure 21.2. Example of the SELECT.

21.3 QUESTIONS/PROBLEMS

Q 21.1: Correct this segment of code.

```
/*REXX sample with errors*/
CASE
    WHEN "NAME" = "JOHN" THEN SAY "GRADE IS 78"
    WHEN  NAME  = "MARY" THEN SAY "GRADE IS 84"
    WHEN  NAME  = "MIKE" THEN SAY "GRADE IS 89"
    WHEN  NAME  = "MONA" THEN SAY "GRADE IS 91"
ELSE  THEN SAY "NOT ON ROSTER"
```

Q 21.2: Are these two segments of code equivalent?

```
/*sample1        */
SELECT
   WHEN  NAME  = "ERIC" THEN SAY "GRADE IS 83"
OTHERWISE  SAY "NOT ON ROSTER"
END
/*sample2 */
IF NAME = "ERIC"
   THEN SAY "GRADE IS 83"
   ELSE SAY "NOT ON ROSTER"
```

Chapter 22

TALKING TO THE ENVIRONMENT

This chapter concentrates on the manner in which you can talk to the operating system that supports TSO, and other command processors that may be available. You will learn how to pass commands to TSO and ISPF, and how to pass commands in the most efficient way possible.

Topics:

22.1 What is "Talking to the Environment?"
22.2 How does REXX know Command is for Environment?
22.3 Who can you talk to?
22.4 When can you talk to them?
22.5 Telling REXX who to Give the Command to
22.6 Is an Environment Available?
22.7 Questions/Problems

22.1 WHAT IS "TALKING TO THE ENVIRONMENT?"

Talking to the environment is what happens when you execute a TSO or ISPF command in a REXX program. REXX understands its own keywords, but doesn't understand the command for the environment. Any command that REXX doesn't understand it passes to the environment, which is usually TSO, but may be ISPF, MVS, the ISPF editor, or other command processors that may have been installed. Whenever a command is passed to the environment, the environment will set the special variable RC to a number to indicate whether the command worked. It will be set to 0 if the command worked, and some other number if the command didn't work. It will be set to minus 3 if the command could not be found. REXX cannot syntax check any command meant for the environment, consequently all environment commands look good to REXX. Errors will be caught by the environment.

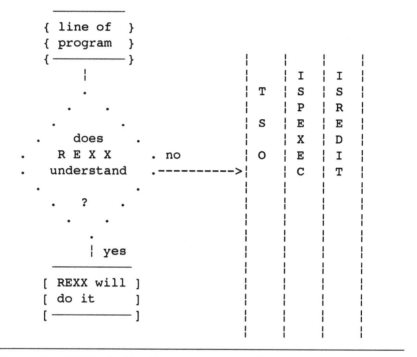

Figure 22.1. REXX decides if a command should go to the environment.

22.2 HOW DOES REXX KNOW COMMAND IS FOR ENVIRONMENT?

REXX looks at every line of the program to decipher each command or instruction. If REXX sees quotes or apostrophes around the first word in the sentence, and the instruction is not an assignment, REXX will pass the command to the environment. An unknown command that is not in quotes or apostrophes will still be passed to the environment, but this action will be less efficient than if apostrophes or quotes were used.

1	is it assignment? do assignment	A = 3
2	is it REXX keyword?	SAY "ahh"
3	is it comparison operator? return a 1 or 0	"abc" = "def"
4	is instruction in quotes? give to environment	"DELETE..."
5	is instruction unknown? give to environment	WHISPER "Hello"

Figure 22.2. How REXX decides if a command is for the environment.

22.3 WHO CAN YOU TALK TO?

TSO: TSO processes TSO commands, such as ALLOCATE and LISTDS. The name of the TSO environment is "TSO".

The ISPF dialogue manager: ISPF provides the ability to display and use custom made panels, to access stored variables, and several other services. The name of this environment is "ISPEXEC".

The ISPF editor: The editor provides the ability to interact with the file being edited. The name of this environment is "ISREDIT".

```
"DELETE ABC.DATA" -------------------------> "TSO"
"ISPEXEC DISPLAY PANEL(PANL123)" -----------> "ISPEXEC"
"ISREDIT (SAVESTAT) = USER_STATE" ----------> "ISREDIT"
```

Figure 22.3. Environments generally available.

22.4 WHEN CAN YOU TALK TO THEM?

You can always pass commands to TSO, from any type of program envisioned
in this book. If you execute your exec from ISPF, you can pass commands to
"ISPEXEC", that is the ISPF dialogue manager, and to TSO. If you execute
your exec from the ISPF editor as a macro, you can pass commands to
"ISREDIT", the ISPF editor, "ISPEXEC", and "TSO". You can always talk to
MVS, because the environment MVS is always there, behind TSO. We will
not discuss talking to MVS in this book.

22.5 TELLING REXX WHO TO GIVE THE COMMAND TO

To talk to TSO, you do not need to do anything special. All commands go to
TSO by default. If you want to talk to another environment, you'll need to
use the ADDRESS command. The address command may be used for a
temporary change in the environment, as shown in Figure 22.5. This allows
you to just execute one command that is intended for a different environment.
This is a temporary change. It sends that command to that environment, but
doesn't change the default permanently. You may also change the default.
See Figure 22.6. This causes all subsequent commands to be sent to the new
environment. You will have to change the default again, to talk to a different
environment.

```
"DELETE ABC.DATA"
```

Figure 22.4. Talking to TSO by default.

```
ADDRESS "environment" "one command for environment"
```

Figure 22.5. How to talk to another environment temporarily.

```
ADDRESS "environment" /* change default */
"command for that environment"
"maybe another command for that environment"

ADDRESS "TSO"            /* back to TSO    */
"command for TSO  "
```

Figure 22.6. How to change the default environment.

```
/*REXX SAMPLE  A1 */

"DELETE ABC.DATA"          /* talk to TSO     */
                           /* by default      */

ADDRESS "ISPEXEC"          /* going to talk to*/
                           /* ISPF from now on*/

"DISPLAY PANEL(ABC)"       /* talk to ISPF    */

ADDRESS "TSO"              /* going to talk to*/
                           /* TSO    again    */

ADDRESS "ISPEXEC" "VGET VAR1 SHARED" /* use variable
                                        services */
```

Figure 22.7. Examples of addressing different environments.

22.6 IS AN ENVIRONMENT AVAILABLE?

You can always ask TSO if an environment is available. The TSO command SUBCOM queries TSO to find out if the desired subcommand environment is active. A Return Code of 0 means the environment is available. Figure 22.8 illustrates asking if an environment is available. Figure 22.9 is an example of asking if the ISPF dialogue manager is available, and sending a command to it if it is.

The exec in Figure 22.10 passes the variable Yournme to the panel which displays it. After the user types in his/her name and presses PF3, control passes back to the REXX exec which can now examine and use the variable Yournme. Details about the installation of this and similar panels are beyond the scope of this book.

```
"SUBCOM environment
IF RC = 0
    THEN ok to address environment
```

Figure 22.8. Asking if an environment is available.

```
"SUBCOM ISPEXEC"
IF RC = 0
THEN
    DO
        ADDRESS "ISPEXEC" "DISPLAY PANEL(PANEL1)"
    END
"SEND 'COMMAND WORKED' U(*) "
```

Figure 22.9. Example of sending a command to ISPF dialogue manager, if it is available, then sending a command to TSO.

```
%           SAMPLE PANEL
%
%
%           TYPE YOUR NAME HERE _YOURNME +
%
```

Figure 22.10. Example of rudimentary Dialog Manager panel that displays REXX variable Yournme, accepts user's input, and passes it to the REXX exec.

22.7 QUESTIONS/PROBLEMS

Q 22.1: Will this line of instruction be passed to
the environment?

Pull var1 var2 var3

Q 22.2: Will this line of instruction be passed to
the environment?

ARTICULATE "PLEASE ENTER NAME "

Q 22.3: If this command works, what will be in RC?

"DELETE ABC.DATA"

Q 22.4: Can you always talk to ISPF from any Exec?

Problem 22.5: Write an Exec to copy your setup exec
(any dataset will do)
to the dataset: TEMP.COPY.DATA
Pass this command to TSO:
COPY REXXPRGS.EXEC(SETUP) TEMP.COPY.DATA NONUM

(The NONUM operand needed to assure a true copy)
If the return code is zero, then issue the
TSO command LIST TEMP.COPY.DATA
Note: Both commands are optional program products.
Your installation may not have them.

Problem 22.6: See if ISPF is available.
If so, then browse your setup exec.
The command to do that is:
BROWSE DATASET(the-dataset)
pass it to the ISPEXEC environment

If not, use the TSO command LIST to view it.
The command to do that is:
LIST dataset

To test it, execute it once inside of ISPF,
once outside.

Q 22.7: Is the environment ISPEXEC always available?

Chapter 23

BUILT-IN FUNCTIONS

In this chapter, you will get acquainted with the more important functions in REXX. Let me remind you at this point that there is a complete list of REXX functions in Appendix B. It is especially important to study the examples and to do the computer problems in this chapter.

Topics:

23.1 How Functions Work
23.2 A few Functions
23.3 Functions Peculiar to TSO
23.4 TSO Examples
23.5 Pitfall with Functions
23.6 Questions/Problems

23.1 HOW FUNCTIONS WORK

Functions are a built-in feature of REXX. REXX supports a very large number of functions that can greatly simplify your programming. A function acts mathematically, or does string manipulation on the data passed to it. The result of the function's action is substituted for the function invocation. This means, that if you write SAY LENGTH("ABCD") in your program, REXX will convert this to SAY 4. Figure 23.1 shows the syntax of a function invocation in REXX. Please note that there may not be a space between the name of the function and the left parenthesis following it.

When two or more elements of data are passed to the function, they are separated by commas, not spaces. Some functions have defaults, and need nothing in parentheses, for example: SAY TIME(). See Figures 23.3, 23.4, and 23.5 for several examples of functions and the results they produce.

All REXX built-in functions may be called like subroutines too. When this is done, the answer is placed in the special variable RESULT. Figure 23.2 shows the syntax of a subroutine call.

143

Note that you may use quotes around the function name. Quotes mean that it is a built-in or external function, not an internal user-written function. SAY "LENGTH"("ABCD") is as valid as SAY LENGTH("ABCD").

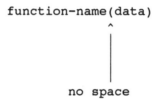

Figure 23.1. How a function is invoked in REXX.

```
CALL function-name data
SAY RESULT
```

Figure 23.2. How a subroutine is invoked in REXX.

```
SAY LENGTH("ABCDE")            /* 5      */

CALL LENGTH "ABCDE"
SAY RESULT                     /* 5      */

SAY TIME()                     /*11:21:43*/
SAY DATE()                     /*09/09/92*/
SAY REVERSE("ABCDEF")          /*FEDCBA  */
SAY RIGHT("ABCDE",3)           /*CDE     */

CALL RIGHT "ABCDE",3
SAY RESULT                     /*CDE     */
```

Figure 23.3. Examples of functions.

23.2 A FEW FUNCTIONS

The full list of REXX functions can be found in Appendix B. I have listed only the more significant ones here. Please examine Figures 23.4 and 23.5 for descriptions of these functions. I will comment briefly on several of them.

DATATYPE (Figure 23.4)
It is absolutely imperative that you check all numbers typed in at the terminal for validity. An example of how this is done is in Figure 23.6.

LENGTH (Figure 23.4) will tell you the total number of characters in the string. If a variable is used, the contents of the variable are examined. Figure 23.15 contains an example of this function.

POS (Figure 23.4) can be used to determine if a character is present. An example of its use is in Figure 23.15.

QUEUED() (Figure 23.5) will return the number of lines that are currently available in the stack. The chapter on the stack (Chapter 27) will provide examples of its use.

SUBSTR (Figure 23.5) will give you a portion of a string. An example of its use is in Figure 23.15.

Please examine Figure 23.7 for an example of how you might create a Hexadecimal addition exec using REXX functions.

```
DATATYPE(string)    result is NUM if a valid REXX number.
                    CHAR otherwise
                    SAY DATATYPE(123) --> NUM
                    SAY DATATYPE(ABCD) --> CHAR

DATE()              date in the format 8 Mar 43

ERRORTEXT(RC)       gives the text of REXX's error
                    message for to error code RC
                    RC is set by any syntax error

LENGTH(string)      counts the characters in string

LINESIZE()          returns the terminal line length

POS(needle,haystack[,start-pos])

                    returns the starting position of
                    needle in haystack
                    if not there, a 0 is returned
                    if start-pos specified,
                    search starts at that position

                    SAY POS('C','ABCDEF') --> 3
```

Figure 23.4. Some functions. Part 1 of 2.

```
QUEUED()        the number of lines available in the stack
                PUSH 'ABCDEF'
                SAY QUEUED() --> 1

SOURCELINE(number)  returns the text of the program
                    source numbered with number
                    /*2 LINE REXX PROGRAM*/
                    SAY SOURCELINE(2) --> SAY SOURCELINE(2)

SUBSTR(string,start-pos,end-pos)
                    returns a portion of a string
                    beginning at start-pos, ending at end-pos
                    SAY SUBSTR('ABCDEF',3,5) --> CDE

TIME()          returns the current time in format hh:mm:ss

USERID()        returns the userid of the person logged on
                and running the Exec
```

Figure 23.5. Some functions. Part 2 of 2.

```
/* REXX sample   make sure person enters a number */
   Arg Num1 .
   If Datatype(Num1) = "NUM"
   Then
      do
        Nop
      end
   Else
      do
        Say "You must enter a number"
        Exit
      end
```

Figure 23.6. Example of making sure a valid number is entered.

```
        /*REXX Hex   adder */
     ARG HEX1 HEX2
     DEC1 = X2D(HEX1)
     DEC2 = X2D(HEX2)
     DECSUM = DEC1 + DEC2
     SAY "HEX SUM IS: " D2X(DECSUM)
```

Figure 23.7. Doing Hex addition using functions.

23.3 FUNCTIONS PECULIAR TO TSO

These functions are available only under TSO. Please examine Appendix B for a fuller description of the TSO functions. I will describe several of them here briefly.

LISTDSI (Figure 23.8). Please note that the three ways shown of expressing the dataset name are equivalent. Refer to the line containing 'SYS1.PROCLIB' for the proper way to put apostrophes around the dataset name when apostrophes are needed. LISTDSI provides a very convenient way of determining whether a dataset exists or not. It would be very gauche (not user-friendly) to allow an exec to end with an error because a dataset does not exist. Figure 23.12 provides an example of LISTDSI. Besides determining if a dataset exists, LISTDSI will provide a wealth of information on it. Please refer to Appendix B for further information.

MSG (Figure 23.8) will tell you what the current setting is, and allow you to change it. It controls whether TSO commands display messages or not. You may use it to control superfluous messages, as from a FREE TSO command that was not needed. This is equivalent to CLIST CONTROL MSG/NOMSG.

OUTTRAP (Figure 23.8) allows you to capture the message normally displayed by a TSO command. This allows you to better format the message, or simply to make use of the information returned, rather than allow it to be displayed at the terminal. An excellent example of its use is in Figure 23.13. See also Figure 23.10.

PROMPT (Figure 23.9) is covered more fully in the chapter on Dialoguing with the Terminal.

SYSDSN (Figure 23.9) is an alternate way of determining if a dataset exists. See Figures 23.11 and 23.13 for examples of its use.

SYSVAR (Figure 23.9) allows you to ask TSO for information it maintains about the current execution environment of your program. SYSVAR provides the same information as CLIST functions such as &SYSENV, &SYSUID, &SYSPREF. See Figure 23.14 for an example of SYSVAR.

LISTDSI

```
CODE = LISTDSI(ABC.DATA)      <─┐
CODE = LISTDSI('ABC.DATA')    <─┼── Equivalent
CODE = LISTDSI("ABC.DATA")    <─┘
CODE = LISTDSI("'SYS1.PROCLIB'")
```

```
          returns a code of
          0  if dataset is OK
          4  if directory information is not valid
          16 if no information is available
             Sets variables also: See Appendix
```

MSG

```
Hold_msg = MSG("ON")
             Capture the setting of MSG
             (Messages generated by TSO commands)
             and change it to ON
```

OUTTRAP

```
Dummy = Outtrap("output_line.","*")
             Capture all messages generated
             by subsequent TSO commands
             Messages are not displayed
             output_line.0 = how many lines
             output_line.1 = the first line
             output_line.2 = the second line
             To supress output altogether:
             Dummy = Outtrap("dummy2",0)
             To go back to normal: DUMMY=OUTTRAP("OFF")
```

Figure 23.8. Some TSO Functions. Part 1 of 2.

```
PROMPT      Hold_prompt = Prompt("ON")
            Capture the current setting of PROMPT
            and change it to ON
            Note: TSO PROFILE must be set to PROMPT
            for this to work. Do this first:
            "PROFILE PROMPT"

SYSDSN      Does the dataset exist?
            If Sysdsn("mylib.cobol") = "OK"
            then .....etc

SYSVAR      Retrieve information retained by the system
            Say Sysvar("SYSPREF")   --> dataset name prefix
            Say Sysvar("SYSPROC")   --> logon procedure
            Say Sysvar("SYSUID")    --> logon userid
            Say Sysvar("SYSISPF")   --> ACTIVE/NOT ACTIVE
```

Figure 23.9. Some TSO functions. Part 2 of 2.

23.4 TSO EXAMPLES

```
/* REXX exec that captures the output of a command*/
   Dummy = Outtrap("CMD_output_line.","*")
   "LISTALC STATUS"
   Say "This many lines were captured:"
   Say  output_line.0
   DO I = 1 to CMD output line.0
       Say "Line of output was:"  output_line.I
   END
```

Figure 23.10. Capturing the message output of a TSO command.

```
/* REXX sample. make sure the dataset name
   entered is really there */
   Arg Dataset_name
   If Sysdsn(Dataset_name) =   "OK"
   Then
      do
        Nop
      end
   Else
      do
        Say "Dataset does not exist"
        Exit
      end
```

Figure 23.11. Example of making sure the dataset name entered exists.

```
If Listdsi(Dataset_name) = 0
Then
   do
     Nop
   end
Else
   do
     Say "Dataset does not exist
     Exit
   end
```

Figure 23.12. Example of making sure the dataset name entered exists, another way.

```
/* REXX sample. make sure the dataset name
   entered is really there
   Do a LISTDS on the dataset, but capture
   the display.  Display the lines of output*/

Arg Dataset_name
If Sysdsn(Dataset_name) =  "OK"
Then
     do
       Nop
     end
Else
     do
       Say "Dataset does not exist
       Exit
       end

Dummy = Outtrap("output_line.","*")
"LISTDS " Dataset_name
Say "This many lines were captured:"
Say output_line.0
DO I = 1 to output_line.0
  Say "Line of output was:" output_line.I
END
```

Figure 23.13. Example of capturing the message output of a TSO command.

```
/* REXX sample. if ISPF is active,
   invoke panel display
   otherwise, start Dialog Mgr */
If Sysvar("SYSISPF") = "ACTIVE"
Then
   do
      Say "Dialogue Manager active, displaying panel"
      ADDRESS "ISPEXEC" DISPLAY PANEL(panel-name)"
      Exit
   end
Else
   do
      Say "ISPF not active, starting with ISPSTART"
      "ALLOC DSN(your-panel-lib-name) DDNAME(ISPPLIB)",
      "SHR REUSE"
      "ISPSTART PANEL(panel-name)"
   end
```

Figure 23.14. Example of checking to see if Dialogue Manager services are available. If so, display a panel. Else start ISPF.

```
/* REXX sample.  Normalize dataset name
  for JCL */
  ARG TSO_Dsn
/* person will key in dataset name with apostrophes,
if TSO's naming conventions require
Example:
%sample   'SYS1.PROCLIB' */
First_apost = POS("'",TSO_Dsn)
Last_apost  = POS("'",TSO_Dsn,2)

If First_apost = 0 &   Last_apost = 0
Then
   do
     /* no apostrophes included in name */
     JCL_Dsn = USERID()    || "." || TSO_dsn
     Exit
   end
If First_apost = 1,
 &   Last_apost = Length(TSO_Dsn)
Then
   do
     /* Apostrophes in name */
     L = Last_apost - 2
     JCL_Dsn = Substr(TSO_Dsn,2,L)
     Exit
   end
Say "Use this name in your JCL" JCL_dsn

If First_apost > 1,
 &   Last_apost = 0
Then
    do
     /* bad name            */
     Say "Invalid dataset name. Terminating"
     Exit
    end
```

Figure 23.15. Example of how to normalize dataset names for JCL. A person entering a dataset name into an Exec must use standard TSO naming conventions regarding apostrophes. JCL doesn't know these conventions.

23.5 PITFALL WITH FUNCTIONS

There is one thing to watch out for, when you use functions. Be careful that you do not leave a space after function-name and before the parenthesis. If you do that, you don't get a function call, you get concatenation. Figure 23.16 shows an example of this pitfall.

```
/*not to do*/

SAY LENGTH ("ABCDEF")
/*gives LENGTH ABCDEF  */
```

Figure 23.16. Example of a pitfall in using functions.

23.6 QUESTIONS/PROBLEMS

Q 23.1: There must be a space after the name of the
function, and before the parenthesis
when you use a function. Yes/No

Q 23.2: When you call a built-in function with CALL
where is the answer given?

Problem 23.3: Accept 2 numbers from the terminal. Check to be
sure they are valid numbers. Subtract one from
the other. Drop the sign of the answer,
display the answer.
The required function can be found in Appendix B.
Expected results:
= = = > %myexec 100 20
80
= = = > %myexec 20 100
80

Problem 23.4: Use Sysdsn to see if there exists a dataset
named WORKSHOP.TEMP
If so, delete it
if not, allocate a new one like your Exec library
The TSO command is:
ALLOC DSN(WORKSHOP.TEMP) LIKE(REXXPRGS.EXEC)

Problem 23.5: Redo the previous one, supressing any display message
from the DELETE command, by using OUTTRAP

Problem 23.6: Redo the previous one, supressing any display message
from the DELETE command, by using the MSG function.

Problem 23.7: Using a function, create an exec that will
convert one character string to another.
Set it up so that if you
type in
ES BUENO
it will print out
IT'S NICE
The required function can be found in Appendix B.

Problem 23.8: Write an exec that will accept a hex number,
a plus or minus sign, and another hex number,
then add or subtract based on the sign.
Display the answer in hex.
Expected results:
= = = > %hexmath e - 2
C
= = = > %hexmath e + 2
10

Chapter 24

USER-WRITTEN FUNCTIONS/SUBROUTINES

This chapter will show you how custom made functions are essentially the same as custom made subroutines. You will learn how to create and use both the internal and external types.

Topics:

24.1 CONSIDERATIONS IN WRITING FUNCTIONS/SUBROUTINES

All built-in REXX functions may be used as functions or subroutines. Please see the chapter on built-in functions for examples of that. I would like to strongly suggest that you write yours so they can be used as either functions or subroutines. It is not hard to accomplish that. You just need to be sure that you always pass information to it through an ARG, that you give back an answer on the RETURN statement, even if it is only the null string, and that you avoid sharing variables with the main part of the program. The benefit of doing things this way, is that you may use your function/subroutine internally or externally with little change, your programs will be more modular and robust. Furthermore, you will be emulating REXX's built-in functions. The seemingly infinite number of hours spent debugging programs written in a Basic that allowed subroutines to share variables with the main part of the program taught me the value of hiding a subroutine's variables from the main part of the program. I urge you to avoid traditional subroutines in REXX. A traditional subroutine shares variables with the main part of the program, it doesn't use ARG, and doesn't RETURN a value.

A REXX function/subroutine can be internal, physically contained in the same program, or external, a separate program. REXX will look internally first, then as built-in, then externally. You may force REXX to look for a built-in, then externally by putting the name of the function/subroutine in quotes. SAY "MYSUBR"(12345) would make REXX search for a built-in, then externally. SAY MYSUBR(1234) would make REXX search internally, then for a built-in, then externally.

Your installation can create a library of functions/subroutines that all REXX programs can use. These same functions/subroutines can be invoked from the QMF (Query Management Facility) FORM panel, and can help immensely in creating custom reports from DB2 data bases.

24.2 WHAT ARE INTERNAL ONES LIKE?

```
/*main part of program */
           .
invoke function/subroutine
           .
           .
EXIT

label:    PROCEDURE
           /*comment explaining purpose*/
ARG var1 var2 var3 var4 ......
/*compute answer here */
RETURN answer
```

Figure 24.1. General form of internal function/subroutine.

Refer to Figure 24.1 for the general form of the function/subroutine, and to Figure 24.2 for an example. User-written internal functions/subroutines are contained within the program. They are usually placed at the physical end of the program, after an EXIT statement, so that control will not fall through into the subroutines. A function/subroutine is defined by a label, which is its first statement. Data is passed to the function/subroutine through its ARG statement. The ARG statement functions like the ARG in the main program, but you may use commas in the function/subroutine to separate the different items of data, and I recommend you do so. After computing the answer, place the answer on the RETURN statement. I strongly suggest you use PROCEDURE after the label to prevent sharing of variables. (See Figure 24.2, and 24.4) Variables are shared if you don't specify PROCEDURE (Figure 24.3). If you use PROCEDURE, and absolutely need to share selected variables, use EXPOSE (see Figure 24.5).

An internal function/subroutine inherits these settings from the main program: ADDRESS, NUMERIC DIGITS, and FUZZ. However, any change that the internal function/subroutine makes to these settings affects only the internal function/subroutine, REXX restores them at the RETURN, so that the main program will see the settings just as it left them. If you want to know the line number of the statement that called the function/subroutine, examine the special variable SIGL. See Figure 24.10 for an example of an internal function/subroutine. This may be compared with Figure 24.11, which is the same function/subroutine done as external.

24.3 EXAMPLES OF INTERNAL

```
/*main program*/
CALL ADDEMUP 1,2         /* invoking with CALL*/
SAY RESULT               /* answer in RESULT   */
EXIT                     /* don't drop into it*/

  ADDEMUP: PROCEDURE     /* label is name        */
                         /* don't share varbls */
  ARG NUM1,NUM2          /*pick up info on args*/
  ANSWER =   NUM1 + NUM2
  RETURN ANSWER          /* give back answer     */
                         /* on RETURN            */
```

Figure 24.2. Example of an internal function/subroutine that doesn't share variables.

```
/*main program*/
CALL ADDEMUP 1,2          /* invoking with CALL*/
SAY RESULT                /* answer in RESULT  */
SAY NUM1                  /* you can do this   */
                         /* because vars shard*/
EXIT                      /* don't drop into it*/


ADDEMUP:                  /* label is name     */
                         /* do    share varbls */
ARG NUM1,NUM2             /*pick up info on args*/
ANSWER =   NUM1 + NUM2
RETURN ANSWER             /* give back answer   */
                         /* on RETURN          */
```

Figure 24.3. Example of internal function/subroutine that shares variables.

```
/*main program*/

SAY  ADDEMUP(1,2)         /* invoking as functt*/
EXIT                      /* don't drop into it*/


ADDEMUP: PROCEDURE        /* label is name     */
                         /* don't share varbls */
ARG NUM1,NUM2             /*pick up info on args*/
ANSWER =   NUM1 + NUM2
RETURN ANSWER             /* give back answer   */
                         /* on RETURN (requird)*/
```

Figure 24.4. Example of internal function/subroutine invoked as function.

```
/*main program*/

CALL ADDEMUP 1,2          /* invoking with CALL*/
SAY RESULT                /* answer in RESULT  */
SAY NUM2                  /* this var shared   */
EXIT                      /* don't drop into it*/


ADDEMUP:                  /* label is name     */
  PROCEDURE EXPOSE NUM2   /* share only num2   */
ARG NUM1,NUM2             /*pick up info on args*/
ANSWER =   NUM1 + NUM2
RETURN ANSWER             /* give back answer  */
                          /* on RETURN         */
```

Figure 24.5. Example of internal function/subroutine that shares only one variable.

2.4 WHAT ARE EXTERNAL ONES LIKE?

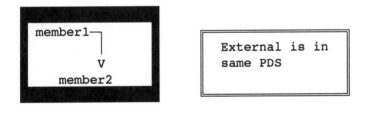

Figure 24.6. External may be found in same PDS.

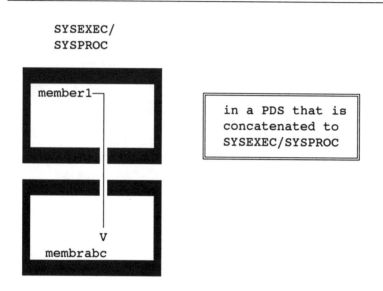

Figure 24.7. External may be found in PDS concatenated to SYSEXEC or SYSPROC.

Examine Figures 24.8 and 24.9. Let us see how external functions/subroutines are different from internal ones. External user-written functions/subroutines are contained in a separate file, and may be a member in the same PDS the main program is in, (Figure 24.6), or a member in a PDS concatenated to SYSEXEC/SYSPROC (Figure 24.7). There is no PROCEDURE statement in external. A label is not used to define the external function/subroutine. All variables are insulated from those of the calling program. Settings of ADDRESS, NUMERIC are not inherited from the caller; they revert to the system default. If you need to exchange variables, you will need to use ISPF variable services.

Similarities with internal. External uses an ARG to pick up the data passed to it. Commas are used to separate the items on the ARG. It ends with a RETURN which passes back the answer to the caller.

See Figure 24.11 for an example of an external function/subroutine. This may be compared with Figure 24.10, which is the same function/subroutine done as internal.

24.5 EXAMPLES OF EXTERNAL

```
/*REXX MAIN PROG */

CALL "ADDEMUP" 1,2            /* invoking with CALL*/
SAY RESULT                    /* answer in RESULT  */
EXIT

- - - - - - - - - - - - - - - - - - - - - - - - - -

/*REXX ADDEMUP   */          /*membername is name */
ARG NUM1,NUM2                /*pick up info on args*/
ANSWER =   NUM1 + NUM2
RETURN ANSWER                /* give back answer   */
                             /* on RETURN          */
```

Figure 24.8. Example of an external function/subroutine invoked as a subroutine.

```
/*REXX MAIN PROG */

SAY   "ADDEMUP"(1,2)      /* invoking as functn*/
EXIT

- - - - - - - - - - - - - - - - - - - - - - - - -

/*REXX ADDEMUP   */       /*membername is name *
ARG NUM1,NUM2             /*pick up info on args*/
ANSWER =   NUM1 + NUM2
RETURN ANSWER            /* give back answer   */
                         /* on RETURN          */
```

Figure 24.9. Example of an external function/subroutine invoked as a function.

```
/* REXX Exec that uses internal subroutine */
FIRST      = 100
SECOND     = 120

/* CALL AS SUBROUTINE */
CALL WHICH_GREATER    FIRST    ,   SECOND
SAY "THE GREATER IS      " RESULT
/* USE AS FUNCTION */
SAY "THE GREATER IS      "
SAY  WHICH_GREATER(FIRST, SECOND)
EXIT

WHICH_GREATER:    PROCEDURE
ARG NUM1, NUM2
IF DATATYPE(NUM1)       = "NUM"
AND DATATYPE(NUM2)      = "NUM"
 THEN NOP
 ELSE RETURN ""

 IF NUM1 = NUM2 THEN RETURN ""
 IF NUM1 > NUM2 THEN RETURN 1
 IF NUM2 > NUM1 THEN RETURN 2
```

Figure 24.10. Example of Internal subroutine to decide which number is greater.

```
/* REXX Exec that uses external subroutine */
FIRST      = 100
SECOND     = 120

/* CALL AS SUBROUTINE */
CALL "WHICHGTR"        FIRST  ,  SECOND
SAY "THE GREATER IS       " RESULT

/* USE AS FUNCTION */
SAY "THE GREATER IS       "
SAY  "WHICHGTR"(FIRST, SECOND)
EXIT
- - - - - - - - - - - - - - - - - - - - - - - - - - - - -

/* REXX Exec WHICHGTR in your exec library */
ARG NUM1, NUM2
IF DATATYPE(NUM1)      = "NUM"
AND DATATYPE(NUM2)     = "NUM"
THEN NOP
ELSE RETURN ""

IF NUM1 = NUM2 THEN RETURN ""
IF NUM1 > NUM2 THEN RETURN 1
IF NUM2 > NUM1 THEN RETURN 2
```

Figure 24.11. Example of External subroutine to decide which number is greater.

24.6 SEARCH ORDER FOR EXTERNAL

If there are no quotes, REXX will search for an internal function, then external. If the function/subroutine name is in quotes, REXX will search for built-in, then external. For further information on the search order, refer to the REXX reference for TSO/E Version 2.

24.7 RECOMMENDATIONS

Hide variables in internal functions/subroutines. If you are invoking an external, put the name in quotes. Use commas to separate items in the ARG, and use commas to separate items passed to the function/subroutine, (see Figure 24.12).

```
CALL RAISE 1000,20

- - - - - - - - - - - - - - -

ARG SALARY,PERCENT
```

Figure 24.12. Using commas on the ARG and the invocation.

24.8 QUESTIONS/PROBLEMS

Q 24.1: In REXX, user-written functions/subroutines
may be used either as functions or subroutines.T/F.

Q 24.2: If you use it as a function, you do it this way
function-name(data). T/F.

Q 24.3: If you use it as a subroutine, you do it this way
CALL function-name data
and the answer comes back in RESULT. T/F.

Problem 24.4: Write an internal function/subroutine that will
concatenate two items passed to it.
(without spaces).
Invoke it as a function, then as a subroutine.
Check automatically within the Exec that both
ways produce the same result.

Expected results:
= = = > %myexec cat dog
INVOKED AS FUNCTION: CATDOG
INVOKED AS SUBROUTINE: CATDOG
RESULTS IDENTICAL

Problem 24.5: Redo the % increase problem as an external
subroutine. Name it PERCENTI.
(See problem 17.4)
Have it accept two parameters
(I.E. arguments). First: Old salary
Second: New salary. Have it return the % increase
on the RETURN statement. Check both numbers
for numeric. If either is not valid, display
a message and return a zero.

Write another exec to test this one, by calling
it as a function, then as a subroutine.

Place both in the same Exec library.

Problem 24.6: Using solution to Problem 24.4 write your
concatenate function/subroutine as an external
function/subroutine.
(leave the internal where it is)
Call the external function/subroutine in such
a way that you are sure to invoke the external
not the internal. Prove that you invoked the
external, not the internal.

Problem 24.7: Create a Metric conversion external subroutine/
function named Metric.
It will accept two arguments: UNIT and QUANTITY
UNIT has these possible values:
    LITER   QUART   MILE   KILOMETER
It returns a number which is the equivalent
of QUANTITY, in the other measuring system,
based upon this table:
1 liter   = 1.057 quarts
1 quart   = .946 liters
1 mile   = 8/5   kilometers
1 kilometer = .625 miles
Also write a main Exec that invokes this
as a function.

Expected results:
= = > %myexec kilometer 1000
    625 MILES

Chapter 25:

EXECUTING ANOTHER PROGRAM

This chapter will point out some things you should be aware of concerning the execution of other programs, written in REXX or CLIST, and how that is different from invoking a function/subroutine.

Topics:

25.1 What does it Mean to Execute Another Program?
25.2 Examples
25.3 Questions/Problems

25.1 WHAT DOES IT MEAN TO EXECUTE ANOTHER PROGRAM?

This is not the same as invoking an external subroutine/function. This is done with an EXEC command, or %membername command. The other program may be written in CLIST or REXX, or other language. A REXX program can pick up information passed to it on its ARG. A CLIST can pick up information passed to it on its PROC. The program can pass back to its caller only one thing: a return code, that is, a number. It cannot pass back a string of characters. A REXX program cannot pick up CLIST GLOBALS, however REXX and CLIST may communicate with each other by means of ISPF variable services.

169

25.2 EXAMPLES

```
/*REXX MAIN    */
"%CHEKIT  FILEA.DATA   "
IF RC = 0
   THEN SAY "FILE FOUND"
```
- -
```
                   /* REXX CHEKIT  */
                   ARG DSNAME
                   IF SYSDSN(DSNAME) = "OK"
                      THEN EXIT 0
                      ELSE EXIT 8
```

Figure 25.1. Example of a main REXX program executing another one.

```
/*REXX MAIN    */
"%CHEKEM  FILEA.DATA        "
IF RC = 0
   THEN SAY "FILE FOUND"
```
- -
```
                   PROC 1 DSNAME
                   /* Clist chekem */
                   IF &SYSDSN(&DSNAME) = "OK" +
                      THEN EXIT CODE(0)
                      ELSE EXIT CODE(8)
```

Figure 25.2. Example of a main REXX program executing a CLIST.

25.3 QUESTIONS/PROBLEMS

Q 25.1: Can the Concat function/subroutine which you created be done as a separate program?

Chapter 26

LOOPING

This chapter will acquaint you with REXX's loop control structure DO. REXX implements the repetition control structure perfectly, allowing many options on the DO. You will see how to repeat and step a variable, set the condition for ending the loop, loop without limit, exit properly from the loop, and how to skip back to the beginning of the loop.

Topics:

26.1 The DO and END
26.2 The DO WHILE
26.3 The DO UNTIL
26.4 Stepping Through a Variable
26.5 Loop Forever
26.6 Skip Back to the Beginning
26.7 Loop a Fixed Number of Times
26.8 Loop Depending on a Variable
26.9 Questions/Problems

26.1 THE DO AND END

The DO control structure always begins with a DO and ends with an END (see Figure 26.1). Between the DO and the END will be found the instructions that are to be executed repeatedly. The loop can be controlled by the addition of modifiers.

```
                               modifiers
    DO     modifiers
           instruction        WHILE
           instruction        UNTIL
    END                       variable =
                              FOREVER
                              FOR
                              number
```

Figure 26.1. General form of the DO and END.

26.2 THE DO WHILE

WHILE continues the loop as long as something is true. It checks before doing the loop the first time, and may not execute the loop even once. See Figure 26.2 for the general form of the DO WHILE, and Figure 26.3 for an example.

```
    DO WHILE something is true
         instructions
    END
```

Figure.26.2. The DO WHILE.

```
    DO WHILE TIME() < "17:01:00"
      SAY "WORK"
    END
```

Figure 26.3. Example of DO WHILE.

26.3   THE DO UNTIL

UNTIL loops up to the moment when something comes true. It checks at the END. It doesn't check before the first time. It will normally do the loop at least once. Figure 26.4 shows the general form of the DO UNTIL. Figure 26.5 is an example of DO UNTIL. Figure 26.6 shows a practical use for the DO UNTIL, in asking for valid information from the person at the terminal.

```
DO UNTIL something is true
        instructions
END
```

Figure 26.4. DO UNTIL.

```
DO UNTIL TIME > "17:00:00"
 SAY "WORK"
END
```

Figure 26.5. Example of DO UNTIL.

```
/* REXX sample. Loop until satisfied with reply */
Valid_reply = ""
DO Until Valid_reply = "YES"
    Say "Please enter a number "
    Pull Number
    If Datatype(Number) = "NUM"
    Then Valid_reply = "YES"
End

Say "Thank you for entering a valid number "
```

Figure 26.6. Example of looping until a valid number is entered.

26.4 STEPPING THROUGH A VARIABLE

Figure 26.7 illustrates stepping through a variable, up to a limit. This puts a 1 into I, and adds 1 to I every time it goes through the loop. When I is more than 10, the loop stops. You may use any variable name you want. If you want to add 2 each time, specify BY 2: DO I = 1 TO 10 BY 2.

You may also step through a variable without a limit. Figure 26.8 illustrates this. You will have to stop the loop with LEAVE.

Please note that if you ask REXX to do something impossible like DO I = 1 TO 10 BY -2, REXX will just ignore you, and not do the loop even once.

```
        DO I = 1 TO 10
                SAY "NUMBER OF TIMES THRU LOOP " I
        END
```

Figure 26.7. Stepping through a variable.

```
        DO variable = 1
                ..
        END
```

Figure 26.8. Step through a variable without limit.

26.5 LOOP FOREVER

You may loop without any limit at all. FOREVER will make the loop continue forever. You do have to get out sometime. You will have to use LEAVE. LEAVE exits gracefully from the loop. Do not use SIGNAL to exit from the loop. See Figure 26.9 for an example of FOREVER and LEAVE.

```
DO FOREVER
    IF TIME( ) > "12:01:00" THEN LEAVE
    SAY "IS IT LUNCH YET?"
END
    <
```

Figure 26.9. Loop FOREVER.

26.6 SKIP BACK TO THE BEGINNING

You may want to skip back to the beginning of the loop. ITERATE says "never mind the rest of the loop", it skips the rest, and goes back to the DO for another pass around the loop. Figures 26.10 and 26.11 illustrate the use of ITERATE.

```
           ┌─────────────┐
      v
    DO I = 1 TO 10       │
                      ^
    IF I = 1 THEN ITERATE
    SAY I
    END
```

Figure 26.10. Skipping back to the beginning.

```
DO I = 1 TO 14
      IF I = 13 THEN ITERATE
      SAY "I IS " I
END
output is     1
              2
              3
              4
              5
              6
              7
              8
              9
             10
             11
             12
             14
```

Figure 26.11. Example of skipping unlucky 13.

26.7 LOOP A FIXED NUMBER OF TIMES

If you ever need to loop a fixed, maximum number of times while stepping through a variable you may use FOR. FOR says no matter what else happens, just go through the loop this many times. Figure 26.12 illustrates FOR. If all you need to do is loop a fixed number of times, you may specify a constant. Figure 26.13 illustrates this.

```
DO I = 1.234 TO 9943.2323 BY .3203 FOR 22
   . .
END
```

Figure 26.12. Looping a fixed number of times with FOR.

```
DO 10
 ..
END
```

Figure 26.13. Looping a fixed number of times.

26.8 LOOP DEPENDING ON A VARIABLE

You may loop depending on the value in a variable. It will loop as many times as the number in the variable. Figure 26.14 illustrates this.

```
DO variable
 ..
END
```

Figure 26.14. Looping depending on a variable.

26.9 QUESTIONS/PROBLEMS

Q 26.1 What is the missing word?

```
DO FOREVER
   SAY "WHAT NUMBER AM I THINKING OF. 1-10"
   PULL NUMBER
   IF NUMBER = 7
      THEN
      SAY "STILL HAVEN'T GOT IT"
END
SAY "GOOD GUESS. GOING TO TRY THE LOTTERY NEXT?"
```

Problem 26.2: Write an Exec that asks the user to enter
a series of numbers, but never enter the same
one twice in a row. Limit it to 10 numbers.

Problem 26.3: Write an external subroutine to compute the
square root of a number passed to it. Name it SQRT
It will accept one ARG: the number.
Validate the number. If negative, or not numeric,
display a message, return a zero.
Establish a tolerance of .01 for determining
when to exit the loop.
Establish a loop limit of 50, as maximum times
to do the loop.
Make your guess 1/2 of the number
Repeat this loop loop_limit times
    Make new-guess = (guess + (number / guess)) / 2
    If the difference between new-guess and guess
        is less than the tolerance,
        exit the loop.
    Make guess = new-guess
end-repeat
Return the new-guess to the caller.

Problem 26.4: Set secret-number equal to 13
Write an exec to keep asking the user to enter
a number from 1 to 20 until the secret-number
is guessed. Limit the loop to 10 guesses.

Expected results:
= = = > %myexec
    PLEASE ENTER YOUR GUESS, FROM 1 TO 20
= = = > 2
    WRONG
= = = > 7
    WRONG
= = = > 13
    RIGHT

Chapter 27:

USING THE TSO STACK

This chapter will tell you how the TSO stack works, how to put things onto the stack and take them off. You will learn how to create a stack of your own and to avoid interference with other programs using the stack.

Topics:

27.1   WHAT IS THE STACK?

The stack is a buffer-like storage area managed by TSO. It holds data keyed in at terminal being read by a program, and data that a program has put into it. The stack is shared by subroutines, and other programs that are called. The stack is temporary, it is deleted when you go back to TSO "READY". A program or Exec may put data into the stack for its own later use, or for use by another program executing concurrently. In addition, some TSO commands may use the stack.

27.2 WHO PUTS THINGS INTO THE STACK?

Figure 27.1 shows the instructions that put information into the stack. In addition, keying at the terminal when the keyboard is unlocked puts information into the terminal buffer.

```
EXECIO read   (FIFO)
QUEUE REXX instruction (FIFO)
PUSH REXX instruction (LIFO)
```

Figure 27.1. Commands that put information into the stack.

27.3 WHO TAKES THINGS FROM THE STACK?

Figure 27.2 shows commands that take information from the stack. In addition, several TSO commands may take information from the stack. Finally, I should point out that PARSE EXTERNAL takes information directly from the terminal buffer, and not from the program stack.

```
EXECIO write
PULL
TSO commands that prompt
TSO commands that have subcommands
PARSE EXTERNAL   (from terminal buffer)
```

Figure 27.2. Commands that take information from the stack.

27.4 DESCRIPTION OF THE STACK

Refer to Figure 27.3. The TSO stack is a 2 part stack, it consists of the terminal input buffer, (not the output buffer) and the program stack. The terminal input buffer is sometimes called the console stack. The program stack is sometimes called the program data buffer.

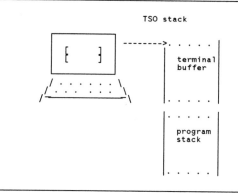

Figure 27.3. The TSO stack. Part 1 of 11.

Refer to Figure 27.4. Data moves in the direction shown, from the top of the stack to the bottom. To aid in understanding and recall, imagine the data carried to the bottom by the force of gravity.

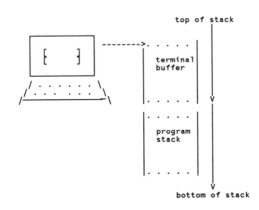

Figure 27.4. The TSO stack. Part 2 of 11.

Refer to Figure 27.5. Data moves one line at a time. Each line in the stack corresponds to one line entered at the terminal, or one REXX instruction being executed. A line may be null, or it may have one word or several. Each PUSH stacks a line, each PULL retrieves a line.

The data that is put on the stack may contain a null, that is zero characters, or one or more character strings.

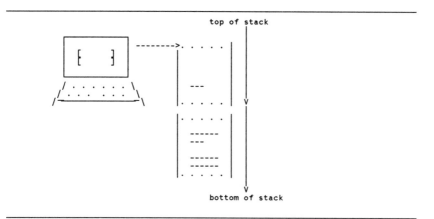

Figure 27.5. The TSO stack. Part 3 of 11.

Refer to Figure 27.6. Terminal input data enters the stack at the top, and proceeds down towards the bottom. Note that since you cannot "type ahead" on TSO, there is normally never more than one line in the terminal input buffer at any given moment. Furthermore, at any time that there is something in the program stack, there is normally nothing in the terminal input buffer.

FIFO commands put data into the program stack as shown on the diagram. Note that data placed into the program stack will reach the bottom before anything that is in the terminal input buffer. Two FIFO commands are: QUEUE and EXECIO READ.

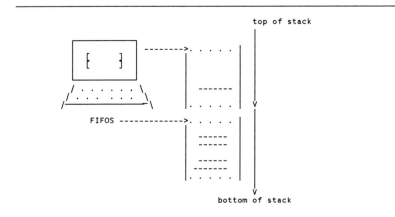

Figure 27.6. The TSO stack. Part 4 of 11.

Refer to Figure 27.7. LIFO commands put data into the stack here. PUSH is a LIFO command. Note that whatever is put into the stack LIFO will be the first thing to reach the bottom.

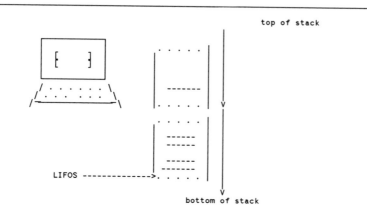

Figure 27.7. The TSO stack. Part 5 of 11.

Refer to Figure 27.8. Data is taken out of the stack where shown in the diagram. Any instruction that takes data out of the stack takes it out from here (except PARSE EXTERNAL). Some instructions that take data out of the stack are: PULL and EXECIO WRITE. If there isn't any data in the program stack, it comes from the terminal input buffer. Figure 27.11 tells you what happens if there is nothing in the terminal input buffer either.

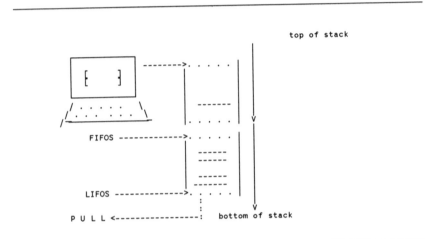

Figure 27.8. The TSO stack. Part 6 of 11.

Refer to Figure 27.9. REXX will tell you how many lines are in the stack with the function QUEUED(). QUEUED() tells you the total number of lines that are available in both the terminal input buffer and the program stack. However, any time you try to count what is in the terminal input buffer, you will get a zero, because data goes from the terminal through the terminal input buffer directly into the instruction that requests the input. It doesn't stay long enough for you to count what's there.

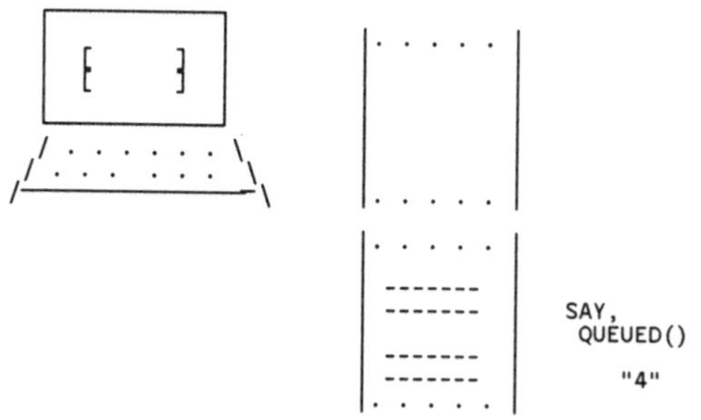

Figure 27.9. The TSO stack. Part 7 of 11.

Refer to Figure 27.10. PARSE EXTERNAL takes data from the terminal input buffer and will not take anything from the program stack. A PARSE EXTERNAL instruction will always unlock the terminal keyboard and you'll always have to type something in in order to continue with your program.

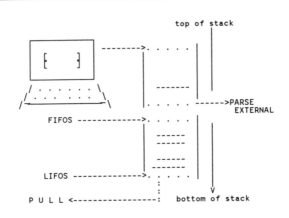

Figure 27.10. The TSO stack. Part 8 of 11.

Refer to Figure 27.11. If the program stack is empty, and you try to take something out of it (with a PULL, for example), TSO will look in the terminal input buffer for a line of input, but won't find it, since you cannot "type ahead" on TSO. The keyboard will then unlock, and TSO will wait for you to type something in.

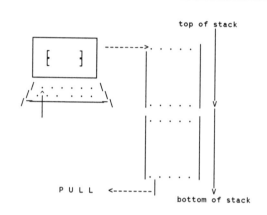

Figure 27.11. The TSO stack. Part 9 of 11.

Refer to Figure 27.12. If your program ends, and all programs that are executing end, control goes back to TSO. If you are executing a macro, control goes back to the Editor. At this time, anything that was left over in the stack will be taken as a command, and TSO will try to execute it! Then the stack is deleted and READY appears on the screen.

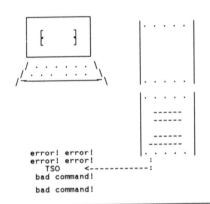

```
error! error!
error! error!
  TSO      <------------:
bad command!
bad command!
```

Figure 27.12. The TSO stack. Part 10 of 11.

27.5 WHAT THE NEWSTACK COMMAND DOES

Refer to Figure 27.13. When you use the NEWSTACK command, the old stack is bypassed, and protected. PULLS pull from the new stack, not the old one. Anything that was in the old stack cannot be accessed, until you do a DELSTACK. Also, anything you may put into the new stack will be deleted when you do a DELSTACK, so you won't interfere with the prior contents of the stack. I recommend you do a NEWSTACK before using the stack, and a DELSTACK after you finish.

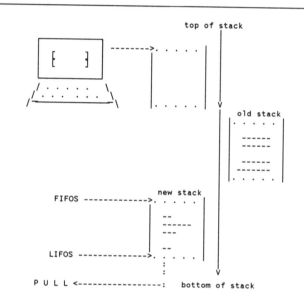

Figure 27.13. The TSO stack. Part 11 of 11.

27.6 RECOMMENDATION ABOUT NEWSTACK

When you use the program stack, and there is any chance that you may communicate with the terminal, or execute other programs that use the stack, you should do what is shown in Figure 27.14. Your program will automatically use the new stack and terminal input will not be affected at all. Be sure to DELSTACK, when finished with your new stack. See Figures 27.15 and 27.16 for examples of NEWSTACK. If you use NEWSTACK before talking to the terminal, you do not need to use PARSE EXTERNAL in place of PULL.

```
            "NEWSTACK"
          use the buffer
        PUSH/PULL/QUEUE/etc

                 .
                 .
          "DELSTACK"
```

Figure 27.14. Recommended action when using the stack.

27.7 EXAMPLES OF NEWSTACK

```
"NEWSTACK"
QUEUE something
PUSH something
EXECIO .....
etc
"DELSTACK"


"NEWSTACK"
QUEUE "ABC.DATA"
"PROFILE PROMPT"
DUMMY = PROMPT("ON")
"DELETE"
etc
etc
"DELSTACK"
```

Figure 27.15. Examples of NEWSTACK and DELSTACK.

```
PUSH "ELEMENT1"
PUSH "ELEMENT2"
NEWSTACK"    /*protects what is already in stack*/
SAY "PLEASE ENTER YOUR NAME"
PULL NAME
SAY "THANK YOU " NAME /*displays name properly*/
"DELSTACK"
PULL STACK_ELEMENT
SAY  STACK_ELEMENT    /* says ELEMENT1" */
PULL STACK_ELEMENT
SAY  STACK_ELEMENT    /* says ELEMENT2" */
```

Figure 27.16. Example of NEWSTACK.

27.8 FUNCTIONS USED WITH THE STACK

If you want to find out how many stacks were created by NEWSTACK, you may use the "QSTACK" command. Subtract one from RC to determine the number of stacks. Refer to Figure 27.17 for an example of QSTACK. Figure 27.18 illustrates a way of deleting all the stacks created by NEWSTACK.

The QUEUED() function, Figure 27.19, 27.20, tells you how many lines are available in the stack, in other words, how many PULLs you can do before the PULL unlocks the terminal keyboard.

```
"QSTACK"
NUM_BUFFS = RC
SAY "THERE ARE " NUM_BUFFS " STACKS "  /* 1 */
"NEWSTACK"
"QSTACK"
NUM_BUFFS = RC
SAY "THERE ARE " NUM_BUFFS " STACKS ALL TOGETHER"/*2*/
"DELSTACK"
```

Figure 27.17. Example of QSTACK.

```
"QSTACK"
How_many = RC - 1
Do How_many
"DELSTACK"
END
```

Figure 27.18. Example of a way to delete all the stacks created by NEWSTACK. Doesn't delete the original stack and what was in it.

```
QUEUED( )        Gives how many lines are now
                 available in the stack
                 that is now being used
                 I.E. How many lines you will get
                 If you keep doing PULLs.
```

Figure 27.19. The QUEUED function.

```
        Say QUEUED( )
        Do QUEUED( )
           Pull line
           Say  line
        END
```

Figure 27.20. Example of using QUEUED() to pull just that many lines from stack.

27.9 EXECUTING A TSO COMMAND THAT HAS SUBCOMMANDS

You may use the stack to communicate with TSO commands that have subcommands.   Some of these commands are: Line mode TSO EDIT, OUTPUT, OPER, and ACF2. The first thing these commands do when they start executing is look in the program stack for input, then if there is nothing there, they issue a read from the terminal causing the terminal keyboard to unlock.

What you must do is stack the subcommands before executing the command. Please note that CLISTs do not work this way. Figures 27.21 and 27.22 illustrate how you stack subcommands.

```
/* REXX sample to prepare subcommands
   for line mode EDIT */
Queue "10 //tsou01a job (accounting),'name',"
Queue "20 //        msglevel=1,class=a"
Queue "30 //        exec pgm=iefbr14"
Queue "40 //dd1      dd dsn=" || Dataset_name || ","
Queue "50 //        disp=shr"
Queue "submit"
Queue "end nosave"
" EDIT TEMPJCL.CNTL NEW EMODE"
```

Figure 27.21. Example of giving subcommands to EDIT through the stack.

```
/* REXX sample for OPER command   */
   Queue "CANCEL U=TSU012"
   Queue "END"
   " OPER"
```

Figure 27.22. Example of giving subcommands to OPER through the stack.

27.10 PASSING INFORMATION TO ANOTHER PROGRAM USING THE STACK

You may pass information to another program by using the stack. The program may be REXX, or assembler. You need to stack the data before executing the program. Figure 27.23 illustrates how you may do this. Figure 27.24 shows a way of explicitly *not* passing information to the program, although there is something in the stack.

```
/* REXX sample to pass data to another program  */
Queue "data line 1"
Queue "data line 2"
%other-program
- - - - - - - - - - - - - - - - - - - - - - - - -
        /*REXX sample "Other Program"*/
        Pull data_line
        Say "received data" data_line
        Pull data line
        Say "received data" data_line
```

Figure 27.23. Example of passing data to a program that is executed.

```
/* REXX sample that DOESN'T pass data to other
   program              */
   Queue "data line 1"
   Queue "data line 2"
   "NEWSTACK"    /*protect current stack*/
   %other-program
   "DELSTACK" /*back to current stack*/
```

Figure 27.24. Example of *not* passing data to a program that is executed.

27.11 QUESTIONS/PROBLEMS

Q 27.1: What will this line of a REXX program do?
        SAY QUEUED()

Q 27.2: There is nothing in either stack.
        Your program says PULL
        What happens?

Q 27.3: Your Exec does 10 PUSHes, and 9 PULLs
        What happens?

Q 27.4: Your Exec does 9 PUSHes, and 10 PULLs
What happens?

Problem 27.5: Accept a dataset name from the terminal
Verify that the dataset name is less than 45 characters long.
Verify that it exists
Place the dataset name into the Stack, so the
LISTDS command can get it
Suggestion: place it LIFO, with PUSH command

Turn on prompting
execute the TSO command LISTDS, but omit the
dataset name, this makes TSO prompt you for it
but it's in the Stack, and LISTDS gets it from there.

Chapter 28:

COMPOUND VARIABLES

This chapter will explain how compound variables are formed and used in REXX. You will learn how to use compound variables to create arrays, and to effect a Random Access Memory.

Topics:

28.1 HOW COMPOUND VARIABLES WORK

Compound variables are a convenient way of grouping variables. They are like arrays in BASIC, and FORTRAN, and like COBOL table handling. REXX EXECIO can use compound variables, and some TSO functions return information in compound variables. Compound variables allow you to name and access several separate items of data by changing just a part of a variable name.

28.2 THE COMPOSITION OF COMPOUND VARIABLES

Compound variables consist of a stem and an extension. The stem is the constant, unchanging part, the solid part of the compound variable. The extension is the part that you can change, to refer to different items of data. A period is used to separate the two parts.

REXX examines the extension part to see if it is a variable. If it is a variable, REXX substitutes its value. Then it looks to see if the combination

199

of stem and substituted extension is a variable. If so, it retrieves that value. Examine Figure 28.1. In this example, WEEKDAY.1 is being set to "SUNDAY", WEEKDAY.2 to "MONDAY", WEEKDAY.3 to "TUESDAY". WEEKDAY is the stem, 1, 2, 3 are the extensions. Then the variable A is set to 1. Then WEEKDAY.A is examined. REXX looks to see if A is a variable. It is. A contains a 1. So the complete, compound variable name is WEEKDAY.1, which contains "SUNDAY", so "SUNDAY" is displayed.

An advantage of compound variables is that you can easily vary A, with a DO. Refer to Figure 28.2 for an example of how you might step through values of A in a loop, and thus refer to different elements in the array. This will set WEEKDAY.1 through WEEKDAY.7. Figure 28.4 shows how you can use a compound variable as an array and how you can fill it with values, and then display those values.

An unusual feature of REXX is that the extension may be a variable that contains a character string. Figure 28.3 is an example of how this might be done. Figure 28.5 is a complete example of this too. It instantaneously retrieves the information that you have typed in. For a very interesting demonstration of what REXX can do, I invite you to type it in, very carefully, and to execute it.

```
WEEKDAY.1       = "SUNDAY"
WEEKDAY.2       = "MONDAY"
WEEKDAY.3       = "TUESDAY"

A = 1
SAY WEEKDAY.A
/* displays SUNDAY */
```

Figure 28.1. Example of the use of a compound variable.

```
DO A = 1 TO 7
    SAY "ENTER DAY OF WEEK"
    PULL WEEKDAY.A
END
```

Figure 28.2. Stepping through values of the extension.

```
Student = "BILL"
Grade.Student = 92
Student = "LOU"
Grade.Student = 89
Student = "MOE"
Grade.Student = 71
Say "Whose grade do you want? (Bill, Lou, Moe)
Pull Who
Say "The grade for " Who " is " Grade.Who
```

Figure 28.3. Using character strings in the extension.

28.3 EXAMPLES

```
/* REXX sample to load an array
   with lines typed in */
Do I = 1 to 20
   Say "please enter a line "
   Pull Element.I
End

/* Unloading the array */
Do I = 1 to 20
   Say Element.I
End

/* Unloading the array in reverse order*/
Do I = 20          to 1 by -1
   Say Element.I
End
```

Figure 28.4. Example of loading and unloading an array.

```
/*random access memory */
DO 100 /*ask names and ages*/
    SAY "WHAT IS YOUR NAME? ('END' TO STOP) "
    PULL NAME
    IF NAME = "END" THEN LEAVE
    SAY "THANK YOU, " NAME ", HOW OLD ARE YOU?"
    PULL HOW_OLD
    IF DATATYPE(HOW_OLD) <> "NUM"
    THEN
        DO  /* NOT A GOOD NUMBER */
            SAY "REJECTED, NOT GOOD NUMBER "
        END
    ELSE
        DO /*GOOD NUMBER */
           AGE.NAME = HOW OLD
        END    /*GOOD NUMBER */
END /*ASK NAMES */

/* NOW ALLOW PERSON TO INQUIRE */
DO 100 /*RETRIEVE AGES*/
    SAY "WHOSE AGE DO YOU WANT TO KNOW?" ,
        " ('END' TO STOP)"
    PULL NAME
    IF NAME = "END" THEN LEAVE
    IF SYMBOL('AGE.NAME') <> "VAR"
    THEN
        DO
            SAY "THAT NAME NOT NOW IN MEMORY"
        END /*NOT IN MEM*/
    ELSE
        DO
            SAY NAME " IS " AGE.NAME " OLD "
        END
END /*RETRIEVE AGES*/
```

Figure 28.5. Example of an Exec that uses compound variables to create a form of random access, or content-addressable memory.

28.4 CHANGING THE STEM

The stem is the first part of a compound variable including the period. If you change the stem, you are changing every single element in the array, even elements that haven't been created yet. Another way to understand that surprising feature is that changing the stem sets a default value for any possible uninitialized variable based on the stem. See Figure 28.6.

```
WEEKDAY.       =       "UNKNOWN"
SAY WEEKDAY.99         /*UNKNOWN*/
WEEKDAY.1      =       "SUNDAY"
SAY WEEKDAY.1          /*SUNDAY*/
SAY WEEKDAY.98         /*UNKNOWN*/
```

Figure 28.6. Changing the stem.

28.5 QUESTIONS/PROBLEMS

Problem 28.1: Write an Exec with a loop that sets NUMBER.1
     thru NUMBER.10 to the numbers 101 thru 110
     then loop through the array, displaying
     the contents of NUMBER.1 thru NUMBER.11
     Yes, NUMBER.11, to see what happens.

Problem 28.2: Write a capture Exec, that captures the display
        from TSO commands, in an array, then displays
        the lines of output one at a time.

   Display "Please enter a command"
   Accept the command, into a variable
   Turn on Outtrap, using the array Display_line.
   Turn off Outtrap.
   Display the message:
      "About to display command's output"
   Loop thru the array,
   displaying each line of the command's output

Chapter 29

EXECIO: READING AND WRITING FILES

This chapter will introduce you to the concept of reading and writing files in REXX execs. After reading it you will be able to understand the general considerations involved in using EXECIO.

Topics:

29.1 FUNCTION OF EXECIO

EXECIO is a facility of TSO, and is a TSO command, not a REXX instruction. However, it is of use only within a REXX exec. EXECIO can read and write datasets that are accessible through TSO (See Figure 29.1).

Since EXECIO is a TSO command, TSO will set the special variable RC. RC will hold a return code of 0 if the command worked, a 1 if a write truncated data, a 2 if end of file was reached, and a 20 for any serious error. Before doing the EXECIO, you must do a successful ALLOCATE command. When you need to create a file, you must specify the attributes of the file with the ALLOCATE command. There will be enough examples of ALLOCATE in the following chapters on EXECIO, but if you require further information you may want to refer to my book "MVS/TSO: Mastering Native Mode and ISPF", published by QED, March 1990.

I strongly suggest you FREE your files before ending your program. In order to do this, you must close the files first with the FINIS option, since FREE won't free an open file. Although ending the program will close the files, you won't be able to FREE them in the program that way.

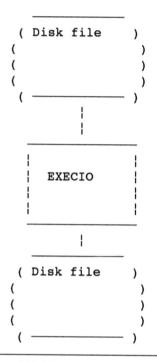

Figure 29.1. The function of EXECIO.

29.2 GENERAL FORM OF COMMAND

```
"ALLOCATE DDNAME(ddname)   DSNAME(dsname)  "

"EXECIO how-many operation  ddname seq (options"
```

Figure 29.2. General form of the command.

Figure 29.2 shows the general form of the EXECIO command. Please note the following. An ALLOCATE is done first. The command is in quotes, since this is a TSO command. "How-many" refers to how many records are to be read or written. It may not be omitted. "*" may be used to stand for the whole file when reading.

There are three possible operations: DISKR-read a record, DISKW-write a record, DISKRU-update a record. "Ddname" stands for the ddname you allocated for this purpose. "Seq" stands for the sequence number of the desired record. Although it is generally omitted, it allows you to skip records on a read, but does not allow you to jump backwards in the file. You may not use it on a write.

There are a few options of interest. First, if you do not specify an option, it means that the stack will be used. If STEM is specified, it means that an array formed with a compound variable will be used. If you wish to close a file, you may specify the option FINIS. You do not need to end the options with a right parenthesis.

29.3 WHAT DO YOU READ INTO?

Refer to Figure 29.3 When you read a file, you may capture the data in two places: the program stack (FIFO) and an array. You may put records in the program stack one record at a time, or the whole file all at once. When using an array, you may read the whole file into it at once.

```
EXECIO READ  --------------------->.  .  .  .  |
                    \                |           |
                      \              |           |
                        \            |           |
                      RECORD.1       |           |
                      RECORD.2       |.  .  .  . |
                      RECORD.n       |           |
```

Figure 29.3. What you can read into.

29.4 WHERE DO YOU WRITE FROM?

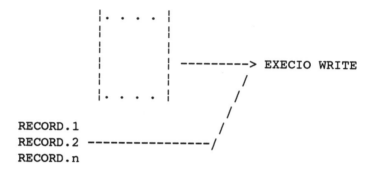

RECORD.1
RECORD.2
RECORD.n

Figure 29.4. What you can write from.

Refer to Figure 29.4. Data may be written from the program stack, or an array. When using the stack, it may be written one record at a time, or the entire contents of the stack at once. When using an array, you must write the whole array at once.

29.5 QUESTIONS/PROBLEMS

Q 29.1: If the EXECIO command works properly, the variable RC is set to what?

Chapter 30

READING FROM A DISK FILE

This chapter details how to read from a disk file. You will see how to read into the stack and into an array.

Topics:

30.1 GENERAL FORM OF COMMAND

Refer to Figure 30.1 DISKR means that you want to read from a disk file. "Ddname" is the DDNAME you used in a prior ALLOCATE command. *"*"* means that you want to read the whole file. If you want to read a certain quantity of records, substitute the number desired for the *"*"*.

```
"EXECIO   *            DISKR  ddname      seq  (options"
```

Figure 30.1. General form of EXECIO for reading.

```
"ALLOCATE DDNAME(INFILE) DSNAME(ABC.DATA) REUSE"
"EXECIO *       DISKR INFILE (FINIS"
```

Figure 30.2. Example of reading whole file into the stack.

30.2 READING WHOLE FILE INTO STACK

Refer to Figure 30.2. The key to reading into the stack is in the options. If you do not specify the STEM option, you get the stack. The FINIS option closes the file after reading it. The *"*"* means that the whole file will be read into the stack. If there is anything in the stack, it will remain, and you won't know what came from the file and what was already there.

Refer to Figure 30.3. This is a fuller example of reading into the stack. Note that "NEWSTACK" is used first. This hides whatever may have been in the stack, so it won't interfere with what you are about to put in the stack from the file. After using the stack, be sure to do a "DELSTACK", to delete the stack you created. The QUEUED() function will tell you how many records are in the stack. You may use that number to control the number of times you loop to PULL what is in the stack.

```
"NEWSTACK"
"ALLOC DDNAME(INFILE) DSNAME(ABC.DATA) REUSE"
"EXECIO * DISKR INFILE (FINIS"
 HOW_MANY = QUEUED()
 DO HOW_MANY
    PULL RECORD
    SAY RECORD
 END
"DELSTACK"
```

Figure 30.3. Example of reading an entire disk file, putting it on the stack, then displaying each record.

30.3 READING ONE RECORD AT A TIME INTO STACK

Refer to Figure 30.4 for an example of putting one record at a time into the stack. The key to this, is the number 1 in the EXECIO command. This reads one record at a time. If you read this way, you'll need to examine RC after each read. When RC becomes a 2 you must stop reading. This example checks for anything other than zero, in case a serious error occurs. It is not necessary to use a subroutine, but it may be more convenient.

```
/* REXX   sample puts one record at a time in stack*/
"ALLOC DSN(INPUT.DATA) SHR REUSE DDN(INFILE)"
"NEWSTACK"
EOF = "NO"
Call Readit

DO I = 1 WHILE EOF = "NO"
    SAY "LINE NUMBER " I " WAS READ "
    PULL RECORD
    SAY RECORD
    Call Readit
END
"DELSTACK"
"FREE DDNAME(INFILE)"

EXIT

READIT:
"EXECIO 1 DISKR INFILE"
IF RC <> 0 THEN EOF = "YES"
RETURN ""
```

Figure 30.4. Example of reading one record at a time and putting it into the stack.

30.4 READING WHOLE FILE INTO ARRAY

Refer to Figure 30.5 Using the STEM option causes the records read to go into an array. When you use the STEM option you must use a period after the stem name. A valid stem name would be "RECD." When you read into an array, REXX puts the first record into stem.1. (RECD.1 if you are using RECD. as a stem name.) The second record goes into stem.2, the third into stem.3, and so on. So you'll know how many records were read, REXX will set stem.0 to the number of records read. If 5 records were read, stem.0 would equal 5, and stem.5 would contain the fifth record.

Figure 30.6 is a fuller example of reading a whole file into an array. The array is then displayed one element at a time, with a DO loop. The variable RECD.0 limits the number of times the loop will repeat.

```
"EXECIO * DISKR ddname     (STEM stem. "
```

Figure 30.5. General form of reading into an array.

```
"ALLOCATE DDNAME(INFILE) DSNAME(TEST.DATA) REUSE"
"EXECIO * DISKR INFILE      (STEM RECD. FINIS"
DO I = 1 TO RECD.0
    SAY "RECORD READ WAS " RECD.I
    /*HERE PROCESS EACH RECORD*/
END
DDNAME(INFILE)"
```

Figure 30.6. Example of reading an entire disk file into an array, and then displaying each record.

Chapter 31

WRITING TO A DISK FILE

This chapter will explain what happens when you write to a disk file, and will explain how you can write from an array and from the stack.

Topics:

31.1 GENERAL FORM OF COMMAND

Refer to Figure 31.1. DISKW means that you are writing to a disk file. "Ddname" is the name you used in a prior ALLOCATE. Note that you may allocate with a NEW keyword, to create the file. In that case you will have to specify the attributes of the file on the ALLOCATE command. You may also allocate with a LIKE, to copy the attributes from another file. (Figure 31.5 contains an example of LIKE.) Finally, you may allocate with MOD, to add new records to the end of an existing file. If you specify neither MOD, nor NEW, nor LIKE on the ALLOCATE, TSO will look for an already existing file. Your first DISKW will start writing at the beginning of the file, destroying any records that may be there.

For "lines" you must use a number that tells how many lines you want to write. This may be a literal, a variable, or the function QUEUED().

"*" may not be used. "*" does not produce the desired results. It writes records until it finds a null line. If it doesn't find one, the keyboard will unlock and whatever you type in at the terminal will be written, until you enter a null line. (Just ENTER).

213

```
"EXECIO lines DISKW ddname (options"
```

Figure 31.1. General form of command.

31.2 WRITING FROM THE STACK

Refer to Figure 31.2. This is the general form of writing all the records that are in the stack to a file. Please note that the variable HOW_MANY is used. QUEUED() could have been used. Figure 31.3 is a fuller example of writing the whole stack to a disk file. Note the use of "NEWSTACK" at the beginning, and "DELSTACK" at the end. This will protect anything that was already in the stack from being written. The FINIS option is used to close the file after writing all the records.

Figure 31.4 is an example of how you might write one line at a time from the stack. The last EXECIO statement is an optional way of closing the file. Note the 0 for number of records, since there are no more records to be written. Figure 31.5 is a way of copying a file to another, using the stack.

```
HOW_MANY = QUEUED()
"EXECIO " HOW_MANY " DISKW ddname(options"
```

Figure 31.2. Writing the whole stack to a disk file.

```
"ALLOCATE DDNAME(OUTFILE) NEW DSNAME(TEST2.DATA)",
" LIKE(TEST.DATA)"
"NEWSTACK"
QUEUE "THIS WILL BE PUT INTO THE FILE"
/*whatever you put on the stack since NEWSTACK
will be written*/
HOW_MANY = QUEUED()

"EXECIO" HOW_MANY     "DISKW OUTFILE (FINIS"
"DELSTACK"
"FREE DDNAME(OUTFILE)"
```

Figure 31.3. Example of writing the whole stack to a disk file.

```
"ALLOCATE DDNAME(OUTFILE) NEW DSNAME(TEST2.DATA)",
" LIKE(TEST.DATA)"
"NEWSTACK"
 QUEUE "THIS WILL BE PUT IN THE FILE"
 /*whatever you put on the stack since NEWSTACK
     will be written*/
 HOW_MANY = QUEUED()
 DO HOW_MANY
     "EXECIO  1            DISKW OUTFILE "
 END

"DELSTACK"
"EXECIO  0  DISKW OUTFILE (FINIS" /*close the file*/
"FREE DDNAME(OUTFILE)"
```

Figure 31.4. Example of writing one line at a time from the stack to a disk file.

```
"ALLOCATE DDNAME(INFILE)   SHR DSNAME(TEST.DATA)"
"ALLOCATE DDNAME(OUTFILE) NEW DSNAME(TEST2.DATA)",
" LIKE(TEST.DATA)"
"NEWSTACK"

"EXECIO  *           DISKR INFILE   (FINIS"
 HOW_MANY = QUEUED()
   "EXECIO" HOW_MANY    "DISKW OUTFILE (FINIS"

"DELSTACK"
"FREE DDNAME(OUTFILE)"
"FREE DDNAME(INFILE)  "
```

Figure 31.5. Example of copying an entire file to another using the stack.

31.3 WRITING FROM AN ARRAY

Figure 31.6 is the general form of writing an array to a file. Note that stem.0 contains the number of records that are in the array, and is used to control how many records are written. Figure 31.7 is a fuller example of how you might write an entire array to a file. Note that the FINIS option is used to close the file after writing the records. Figure 31.8 is an example of how you might copy a file to another, using an array.

```
HOW_MANY = stem.0
"EXECIO" HOW_MANY "DISKW ddname (STEM stem. FINIS"
```

Figure 31.6. Writing an array to a disk file.

```
/*ASSUMING THE ARRAY IS ALREADY LOADED*/
"ALLOCATE DDNAME(OUTFILE) DSNAME(TEMP3.DATA) NEW ",
" LIKE(TEST.DATA)  "

HOW_MANY = RECD.0
"EXECIO"   HOW_MANY "DISKW OUTFILE (STEM RECD. FINIS"
"FREE DDNAME(OUTFILE)"
```

Figure 31.7. Example of writing entire array to a disk file.

```
"ALLOCATE DDNAME(INFILE    SHR DSNAME(TEST.DATA)"
"ALLOCATE DDNAME(OUTFILE) NEW DSNAME(TEST2.DATA)",
" LIKE(TEST.DATA)"

"EXECIO  *   DISKR INFILE   (STEM RECD. FINIS"

"EXECIO" RECD.0 "DISKW OUTFILE (STEM RECD. FINIS"

"FREE DDNAME(OUTFILE)"
"FREE DDNAME(INFILE)  "
```

Figure 31.8. Example of copying a file to another using an array.

31.4 UPDATING A RECORD

EXECIO can update a record in place. It can read a record, allow you to change it, and then rewrite it. Please note that you cannot jump backwards in a file. You may skip records, but only if you go forward. DISKRU tells TSO you will be reading records, and possibly updating them. It is advisable to use OLD in the ALLOCATE, to assure that no one else can access the file while you are updating it. Note that OLD is the default, so if you don't specify SHR, you'll get OLD. Figure 31.9 is an example of updating record number 10, using the stack. Figure 31.10 is an example of updating records in the file, looping through the file.

```
"ALLOCATE DDNAME(INFILE)   OLD DSNAME(TEST.DATA)"
"NEWSTACK"
"EXECIO  1   DISKRU   INFILE 10 "   /* get record */
  Pull Record /* take record out of stack */
  Record =  "abcdefghi" /* change record */
  Push Record /* put record back into stack */
"EXECIO  1   DISKW    INFILE      "  /* rewrite*/
"DELSTACK"
"EXECIO  0   DISKW    INFILE (FINIS " /* close*/
"FREE DDNAME(INFILE)  "
```

Figure 31.9. Example of updating record 10 in a file.

```
/* Rexx   update one record at a time in stack*/
"ALLOC DSN(INPUT.DATA) OLD REUSE DDN(INFILE)"
"NEWSTACK"
EOF = "NO"
Call READIT
DO I = 1 WHILE EOF = "NO"
SAY "LINE NUMBER " I " WAS READ "
PULL RECORD
/* HERE CHANGE RECORD */
PUSH RECORD
Call WRITIT
Call READIT
END
"DELSTACK"
"FREE DDN(INFILE)"
EXIT
READIT:
"EXECIO 1 DISKRU INFILE"
IF RC <> 0 THEN EOF = "YES"
RETURN ""

WRITIT:
"EXECIO 1 DISKW  INFILE"
RETURN ""
```

Figure 31.10. Example of looping through a file, one record at a time, updating records individually.

Chapter 32

PRACTICE PROBLEMS WITH EXECIO

This chapter consists of several computer problems concerning EXECIO that you should try out. They will give you valuable practice with this facility.

Topics:

32.1 Questions/Problems

32.1 QUESTIONS/PROBLEMS

Problem 32.1: Choose a file that you currently have under
   your userid. Read it into an array.
   Display every other record, starting with record 1.

Problem 32.2: Read in a file that you currently have under
   your userid. Read it into an array.
   Write it out to another file.
   Get both file names from the terminal by asking.
   To allocate the new file, use an allocate command
   with LIKE.

Problem 32.3: Read any file of yours into an array
   1 record at a time.
   As you read, count each record. Keep track of
   the length of the longest record
   At the end of the program, display the record count,
   and the length of the longest record.

Problem 32.4: Modify the CAPTURE exec (Problem 28.2)
   to store the lines of the display
   in the dataset TEMP.CAPTURE.DATA
   Use SYSDSN to see if that dataset exists.
   If it exists, delete it.

   Then allocate it (create it), with the following
   TSO command:
   ALLOC DSN(TEMP.CAPTURE.DATA) DDNAME(CAPTURE)
      SPACE(1 1) TRACKS LRECL(80) BLOCK(4000) RECFM(F B)
   (Normally typed in on one line, not two)

   Outtrap loads an array. Use that array to write
   out the lines of the command display.

   The Write command should close the file
   at the same time.

Chapter 33

THE INTERPRET INSTRUCTION

This chapter will help you to understand the functioning of the INTERPRET instruction and suggest some possible uses for it.

Topics:

33.1 WHAT INTERPRET DOES

INTERPRET makes REXX process an expression as an instruction. It says to REXX "have another look". The string that is formed by the expression is reexamined by REXX, which then takes it as a REXX instruction.

Please note that the VALUE function is similar. Before using INTERPRET, check to see if the VALUE function is more suitable. Figure 33.1 shows how two variables containing "SAY" and "HELLO" are examined by the INTERPRET instruction, which then executes the instruction "SAY HELLO".

Figure 33.2 shows what would happen if you simply tried to execute the two variables as an instruction. They would be passed to TSO, which would not recognize the SAY as a TSO command.

Figure 33.3 shows a way of making REXX use a variable that was not in the original program, but is made up of something that was typed in at the terminal.

```
INSTR = "SAY"
VAR = "HELLO"
INTERPRET INSTR VAR    /*becomes SAY HELLO*/
                       /*interpret executes that */
```

Figure 33.1. Example of how INTERPRET processes an expression, or string.

```
INSTR = "SAY"
VAR = "HELLO"
INSTR VAR               /*becomes SAY HELLO*/
                        /*but REXX passes it to */
                        /*the environment,      */
/*command not found*/   /*which rejects it      */
```

Figure 33.2. Example showing what happens if you don't use INTERPRET.

```
SAY "PLEASE ENTER YOUR NAME"
PULL NAME
SAY "THANK YOU, " NAME " NOW ENTER YOUR AGE "
PULL AGE
INTERPRET  NAME "=" AGE
/*if name was JOE, it assigns the variable JOE
   the value of his age*/
SAY "WHOSE AGE DO YOU WANT TO RETRIEVE?. ENTER NAME"
PULL NAME
INTERPRET "SAY " NAME
/*if name was JOE, it executes the instruction
SAY JOE*/
```

Figure 33.3. Example of making REXX find the value of a variable which was not in the original, source, program. A variable equal to whoever's name is typed in is created.

33.2 QUESTIONS/PROBLEMS

Problem 33.1:
    Create a quick calculator exec
    Use **INTERPRET** to execute an expression that is typed in
    Display the result
    Name it CALC

    It will be used this way:
    = = > CALC 1 + 1
    It will display 2

Chapter 34

EDIT MACROS

This chapter will give you the information needed to begin writing macros for the ISPF editor.

Topics:

34.1 What is an Edit Macro?
34.2 Using Edit Macros
34.3 Examples
34.4 Questions/Problems

34.1 WHAT IS AN EDIT MACRO?

An edit macro is a custom written subcommand of the ISPF editor. It may execute edit subcommands, such as "SAVE", special edit macro commands such as CURSOR = 10 4, TSO commands, and REXX instructions. (See Figure 34.1). It must be a member in a library allocated to SYSEXEC or SYSPROC.

34.2 USING EDIT MACROS

An edit macro is executed as if it were a subcommand of edit. You just type its name on the command line. For example, if there were a macro named TRUNC in a library allocated to SYSEXEC, you would just type %TRUNC on the command line.

The very first statement after the initial comment must be a command that tells the editor that this is a macro. That is the ADDRESS "ISREDIT" "MACRO PROCESS" command shown in Figure 34.1.

If no parameters are to be passed to the macro, use the command as shown. If parameters are to be passed to the macro, place the names of the parameters within parentheses as shown in the ADDRESS "ISREDIT" "MACRO" statement in Figure 34.2. A parameter is passed to the macro just as arguments are passed to a regular REXX exec. So, to pass the desired userid to the macro in Figure 34.2, you would type the userid next to the name of the macro when executing it, for example %macroname USERID. (See Figure 34.3). In Figure 34.2 USERID is a parameter representing the userid of the person who is to receive the message. Later on in the exec, USERID is used as an ordinary REXX variable in the SEND command.

The word PROCESS means that the macro will be executed after all the ISPF edit line commands that are on the screen are processed. You may change this to NOPROCESS in order to execute the macro before the ISPF edit line commands.

Recall that the default environment is TSO, so there is no need to do anything special to talk to TSO. However, to pass a command to the editor, you must prefix it with ADDRESS "ISREDIT". You will see in all the examples that edit subcommands are prefixed with ADDRESS "ISREDIT", and that the rest of the edit subcommand is bounded in quotes.

Please notice that variables are placed in parentheses when used in edit subcommands. In Figure 34.2 MEMB is a variable, and so when used in an edit subcommand it is in parentheses.

34.3 EXAMPLES

```
/*REXX Editor macro that changes all lower case to
   upper and sends a message to your friend       */
ADDRESS "ISREDIT" "MACRO PROCESS"
ADDRESS "ISREDIT" "CHANGE P'<' P'>' ALL"
"SEND 'HI SUE' U(TSOU02)" /*note: TSO command */
/*G. F. Gargiulo 5   9 90                         */
```

Figure 34.1. Edit macro that changes all lower case to upper.

```
/* REXX sayhi  macro illustrates edit subcommand
   and TSO command */
/* USER ID is picked up as a parameter, just like
   an ARG in regular execs */
/* MEMB is the variable which will hold member name */
ADDRESS "ISREDIT" "MACRO (USERID) PROCESS"
/* USERID is the user id of the person who'll
   get the message */
ADDRESS "ISREDIT" "(MEMB) = MEMBER"   /* GET MEMBER
                                         NAME */
"SEND 'HI. AM EDITING MEMBER " MEMB " USER("USERID")"
```

Figure 34.2. Edit macro that will send message to friend.

```
==> %SAYHI USER02
```

Figure 34.3. Using the macro in Figure 34.2.

228 REXX in the TSO Environment

```
/* REXX macro that illustrates various things that
   work only in macros */

   ADDRESS "ISREDIT " " MACRO PROCESS"

/* get name of edit profile */
   ADDRESS "ISREDIT " "(MYPROF) = PROFILE "

/* save all current edit settings */
   ADDRESS "ISREDIT " "(USTATE) = USER_STATE"

/* restore current edit settings */
   ADDRESS "ISREDIT " "USER_STATE = (USTATE)"

/* get exclusion status of line 5
     X = excluded      NX = not */
   ADDRESS "ISREDIT " "(XSTAT) = XSTATUS 5"

/* simulate Text Split command on line 5, column 3*/
   ADDRESS "ISREDIT " "TSPLIT 5 3 "

/* simulate Text Enter command on line 5 */
   ADDRESS "ISREDIT " "TENTER 5"

/* define an edit mask */
   ADDRESS "ISREDIT " "MASKLINE = 'ABCDEF' "

/* delete line 5 */
   ADDRESS "ISREDIT " "DELETE 5"

/* do an insert after line 5 */
   ADDRESS "ISREDIT " "INSERT 5 "

/* get count of changes made */
   ADDRESS "ISREDIT " "(CCOUNT) = CHANGE_COUNTS"

/* get macro level */
   ADDRESS "ISREDIT " "(MLEV) = MACRO_LEVEL"
```

Figure 34.4. Various macro commands. Part 1 of 3.

```
/* get record length */
    ADDRESS "ISREDIT " "(LREC) = LRECL "

/* change a line of data */
    ADDRESS "ISREDIT " "LINE 5 = 'THIS IS NEW LINE 5'

/* get line number of first line */
    ADDRESS "ISREDIT " "(FLIN) = LINENUM .ZF"

/* get line number of line cursor is on */
 ADDRESS "ISREDIT " "(LCURS) = LINENUM .ZCSR"

/* get line number of last line */
    ADDRESS "ISREDIT " "(LLINE) = LINENUM .ZL"

/* put a label on a line, scroll there */
    ADDRESS "ISREDIT " "(HERE) = CURSOR"
    ADDRESS "ISREDIT " "LABEL " HERE " = .CURRENT"
    ADDRESS "ISREDIT " "LOCATE .CURRENT"

/* execute something only if it's a subcommand */
    ADDRESS "ISREDIT " "BUILTIN CHANGE 'ABC' 'DEF' ALL"

/* change a profile setting */
    ADDRESS "ISREDIT " "STATS = OFF"

/* insert a line after cursor position */
ADDRESS "ISREDIT" "LINE_AFTER .ZCSR = 'INSRT AFTER CUR'"

/* insert a line after first */
ADDRESS "ISREDIT " "LINE_AFTER .ZF = 'INSERT AFTER 1ST'

/* insert a line after last */
ADDRESS "ISREDIT " "LINE_AFTER .ZL = 'INSERT AFTER LST'

/* scroll to cursor position */
    ADDRESS "ISREDIT " "LOCATE .ZCSR"
```

Figure 34.5. Various macro commands. Part 2 of 3.

```
/* save position of cursor */
   ADDRESS "ISREDIT " "(CURLINE,CURCOLM) = CURSOR "

/* restore position of cursor */
   ADDRESS "ISREDIT " "CURSOR = " CURLINE CURCOLM

/* position cursor to line 7 in data, column 46 */
   ADDRESS "ISREDIT " "CURSOR = 7 46 "

/* save dataset name being edited */
   ADDRESS "ISREDIT " "(DSN) = DATASET"

/* save member name being edited */
   ADDRESS "ISREDIT " "(MEMBR) = MEMBER "

/* save display limit of lines */
ADDRESS "ISREDIT " "(FRSTLIN,LASTLIN) = DISPLAY_LINES"

/* save display limit of columns */
ADDRESS "ISREDIT " "(FRSTCOL,LASTCOL) = DISPLAY_COLS"
```

Figure 34.6. Various macro commands. Part 3 of 3.

```
/* REXX SAMPLE MACRO. SHOWS HOW TO DO SOMETHING
   DIFFERENT FOR EACH LANGUAGE TYPE.
   TO USE IT, TYPE ITS NAME ON THE COMMANDLINE */

   "SUBCOM ISREDIT"
   IF RC <> 0
   THEN
       DO
           SAY "MAY BE EXECUTED AS AN EDIT MACRO ONLY "
           EXIT
       END
   ADDRESS "ISREDIT " "MACRO NOPROCESS"

/* save current settings */
   ADDRESS "ISREDIT " "(USTAT) = USER_STATE"
/* save profile name */
/* assume profile name is language type */
   ADDRESS "ISREDIT " "(LANGTYPE) = PROFILE"
/* create back up copy */
   ADDRESS "ISREDIT" "(DSN) = DATASET"
   ADDRESS "ISREDIT " "(MEMB) = MEMBER "
   IF MEMB = ""
   THEN "COPY " DSN " TEMPBKUP.DATA NONUM"
   ELSE
     DO
       IF MEMB <> "BKUPMEMB"
       THEN
           ADDRESS "ISREDIT " "REPLACE BKUPMEMB .ZF .ZL"
     END

   IF LANGTYPE = "COBOL"
   THEN
       DO
           ADDRESS "ISREDIT " "CHANGE P'=' ' ' 73 80 ALL"
           ADDRESS "ISREDIT " "RESET"
       END
/* restore original state */
   ADDRESS "ISREDIT" "USER_STATE = (USTAT)"
```

Figure 34.7. Example of some things you might do with a macro.

34.4 QUESTIONS/PROBLEMS

Problem 34.1: Write an ISPF Editor macro to save and execute
the Exec that you are editing.
Name it Runit
It must start off with the usual comment
then ADDRESS "ISREDIT" "MACRO PROCESS"
Pass this command to the ISPF Editor:
REPLACE TESTXXXX .ZF .ZL
Pass this command to TSO:
EXEC your-exec-library(TESTXXXX) EXEC
It will work with libraries only
To execute it, type RUNIT on the command line
in the editor

Problem 34.2: Enhance problem 34.1. Check to see if you
are trying to execute RUNIT.
Get the member name from the editor.
If the member name is RUNIT, issue message, exit.

Chapter 35

CONVERTING FROM CLISTS

This chapter will provide some help in converting CLISTs to REXX programs. Some considerations involved in converting are discussed. You find a table of CLIST features along with the corresponding features of REXX, with an example of each. You should be aware that many equivalences are only approximate.

Topics:

35.1 CONSIDERATIONS IN CONVERTING

Conversion of one language to another requires a knowledge of both languages and how they function. This book is about REXX, not CLISTs, and will not explain CLIST features in detail. For detailed information about CLISTs I recommend "MVS/TSO: Mastering CLISTs", by Barry K. Nirmal, published by QED.

CLISTs and REXX share many features. Both have good control structures such as DO WHILE. These can usually be converted without any problem.

CLIST GOTO's cannot always be converted to REXX SIGNAL's, because REXX's SIGNAL destroys any loop or control structure it is in. You may have to rewrite the logic of CLIST GOTO's.

Changing the value of a loop variable in REXX affects the outcome of the loop. An example of this is DO I = 1 to 10, and changing the value of I within the loop. CLIST does not function the same way.

REXX has nothing even near GLOBAL variables. You can use ISPF Variable Services to produce the same results.

CLIST examines a program statement and processes it repeatedly until all *"&"* variables are resolved. REXX examines a statement once only, unless you use the INTERPRET instruction. CLIST statements containing variables within variables may severely tax your conversion abilities.

CLIST PROC statement works differently from REXX ARG. There is no one-to-one correspondence. You will have to execute REXX differently, without reliance on keyword parameters.

REXX has no WRITENR which displays a message and leaves the cursor at the end of the line. You might consider using ISPF panels, although this is considerably more involved.

35.2 TABLE OF CORRESPONDING FEATURES

CLIST Features	*REXX Equivalents*
AND IF &A = 1 AND &B = 2	& IF A = 1 & B = 2

ATTN
  ATTN DO
  ...
  END
	Halt trap
	SIGNAL ON HALT

Concatenation by juxtaposition. All spaces remain. WRITE HI NICE DAY! -> HI NICE DAY!	Concatenation by juxtaposition. > 1 spaces become 1 space SAY HI NICE DAY! -> HI NICE DAY
Concatenation with operator. SET &NAME = WILL |+ FRED	Concatenation with operator. NAME = "WILL" || "FRED"
CONTROL LIST	Trace All
CONTROL NOMSG	Dummy = MSG("OFF")
CONTROL PROMPT	Dummy = PROMPT("ON")
CONTROL SYMLIST CONLIST	Trace I

DATA
  LISTCAT
  LISTDS
ENDDATA
	Environment commands in quotes
	"LISTCAT"
	"LISTDS"

DO WHILE	DO WHILE

Error trap
  ERROR DO
  ...
  END
	ERROR, SYNTAX traps
	SIGNAL ON ERROR
	SIGNAL ON SYNTAX

EXIT CODE(number) EXIT CODE(10)	EXIT number EXIT 10
EXIT QUIT	No equivalent
File IO GETFILE INFILE	EXECIO "EXECIO 1 DISKR INFILE"
GLOBAL variables GLOBAL &V1 &V2 + &V3	No equivalent
IF ... AND	IF ... &
IF ... OR	IF ... |
IF (null)	IF ... NOP
GOTO GOTO ENDPROG	SIGNAL label SIGNAL ENDPROG
LISTDSI dsn	Dummy = LISTDSI(dsn)
Literal has no delimiter, or uses &STR() WRITE HELLO	Literal needs no delimiter, or may use ", or '. SAY HELLO
NGLOBAL NGLOBAL VAR1	No equivalent
PROC keyword parameters with default PROC 0 TRACE(NO)	No equivalent
PROC keyword parameters without default PROC 0 TRACE	No equivalent
PROC prompts for positionals PROC 1 VAR1	ARG does not prompt ARG VAR1

PROC statement
PROC 1 VAR1

ARG (approx)
ARG VAR1

READ &var
READ &NAME

PULL (approx)
PULL NAME

READ (goes into &SYSDVAL)
READ
WRITE YOU TYPED IN -
&SYSDVAL

PULL variable
PULL NAME
SAY "YOU TYPED IN",
    NAME

Variable starts with &
WRITE &NAME

Variable has no delimiter
SAY NAME

WRITE and WRITENR
WRITE PLSE ENTER -
NAME

SAY "PLSE ENTER", "NAME"

S E T & L I N E = +
&&SYSOUTLINE&ctr

LINE = SYSOUTLINE.I (in loop
varying I)

SET &SYSOUTTRAP-
= 200

Dummy = OUTTRAP("line.",200)

SET &SYSOUTTRAP = 0

Dummy = OUTTRAP("OFF")

subroutine label: proc 1 var

subroutine label: ARG on next
line
SUBR:
ARG VAR1

subroutine END

subroutine RETURN

subroutine SYSREF
SYSREF VAR1

subroutine EXPOSE (approx)
EXPOSE VAR1

SYSCALL
SYSCALL SUBROUT

CALL
CALL SUBROUT

+ - continuation
WRITE PLEASE +
  ENTER NAME

, continuation
SAY "PLEASE ",
  "ENTER NAME"

&SUBSTR WRITE &SUBSTR(1:3,ABC)	SUBSTR SAY SUBSTR("ABC",1,3)
&LENGTH &LENGTH(ABCD)	LENGTH LENGTH("ABCD")
&LASTCC and &MAXCC set after all instructions	RC set after environment commands
&DATATYPE IF - &DATATYPE(&NUMBER) =- NUM	DATATYPE() IF DATATYPE(NUMBER) =, "NUM"
&SYSDATE, **&SYSTIME** WRITE &SYSDATE	DATE(), TIME() SAY DATE()
&SYSICMD	no equivalent
&SYSOUTLINE	LINE.0 (see OUTTRAP)
&SYSPREF, &SYSPROC WRITE LOGON PROC =+ &SYSPROC	See SYSVAR SAY "LOGON PROC = ", SYSVAR(SYSPROC)
&SYSSCAN	no equivalent
&SYSUID WRITE YOU ARE - &SYSUID	See SYSVAR SAY "YOU ARE ", SYSVAR(SYSUID)

Appendix A:

PROBLEMS AND SOLUTIONS

Chapter 1

Q 1: Can REXX be used to protect the user from his/her errors?

A: Yes, by front ending commands or putting several commands into one program.

Q 2: List three TSO commands that are potentially destructive and could benefit from some protection using REXX.

A: DELETE RENAME LOGOFF CANCEL

Chapter 2

Q 1: What language is this program written in?

```
/*REXX EXEC TO COMPILE MY PROGRAM*/
COBOL PROG1 SOURCE XREF
```

A: REXX

Q 2: What language is this program written in?

```
/*COMMAND PROCEDURE TO COMPILE MY PROGRAM*/
COBOL PROG1 SOURCE XREF
```

A: CLIST

Q 3: If you allocate your REXX program library as follows, how must you execute it?

ALLOC DDNAME(SYSEXOC) SHR DSN(MYPROGS.EXEC)

A: EXEC MYPROGS(MYPROGM)
(Library was not allocated to SYSEXEC)

Chapter 3

Q 1: What 2 significant language features does REXX lack?

A: I-O
Datatyping

Q 2: How is the lack of Input-Output made up for?

A: By the TSO command EXECIO

Chapter 4

Q 1: What must a REXX program always start with?

A: /*REXX.........*/

Q 2: What word, or instruction in REXX means to display upon the terminal?

A: SAY

Q 3: What does this program do?
    /*REXX SAMPLE*/
    X = 10
    Y = 20
    Z = Y - X
    SAY "THE ANSWER IS " Z

A: It displays
THE ANSWER IS 10
upon the terminal.

Chapter 6

Q 1: Create a Sequential REXX Exec named LISTER.EXEC. Place in it these TSO commands:

> LISTCAT
> LISTDS LISTER.EXEC

A: ISPF Option 3.2
   A - Allocate
   Type LISTER.EXEC in "Other" field
   (ENTER)
   primary space 1
   secondary space 1
   directory blocks 0
   space units TRKS
   record format VB
   record length 255
   block size 1680
   (ENTER)
   =2
   (ENTER)
   Type LISTER.EXEC in "Other" field
   I5 on asterisks in upper left
   /* REXX exec problem 6.1 */
   LISTCAT
   LISTDS LISTER.EXEC
     - or -
   "LISTCAT "
   "LISTDS LISTER.EXEC "
   On command line: SAVE
   On command line: TSO EXEC LISTER EXEC

Chapter 8

Q 1: How many directory blocks do you allocate for a sequential Exec dataset?

A: None.

Q 2: How many directory blocks do you allocate for a partitioned Exec dataset that will contain 30 members?

A: Seven or eight.

Q 3: After doing the allocation and concatenation described in this chapter, create an exec named TRYIT, containing this command:
SAY "THIS IS THE TRYIT EXEC"
Execute it this way: %TRYIT

A: Follow the steps in this chapter, then select Edit. Key in the following:

/* REXX exec tryit */
SAY "THIS IS THE TRYIT EXEC"

Chapter 9

Q 1: Are these correct syntax?

A SAY "HELLO";SAY "GOODBYE"

B SAY "HELLO";
   SAY;
   "GOODBYE"

C COMPUTE;   C = 3 + 4

A: A Yes.
   B No.
   SAY,
   "GOODBYE"
   C No.
   COMPUTE: C = 3 + 4

Q 2: A label is the target of an instruction that transfers control to it. T/F?

A: T

Q 3: The instruction EXIT must always be the very last line in the program. T/F?

A: F   Not needed if it would be the last line.

Q 4: Will REXX try to execute this line?
BARK "HELLO"

A: No. REXX doesn't understand the word "BARK", so it gives it to TSO.

Q 5: Write an Exec to execute the TSO commands:
TIME
send 'sample exec ' user(*)
Include the comment:
This is a sample Exec for REXX class
Execute the REXX command:
Say TIME() DATE()
But use two lines and a continuation character.
Expected results:
= = > %p0905
09:05:02 03/08/42 CPU 4.3 SVC 888.323
+ SAMPLE EXEC TSOU01
09:05:02 03/08/42

A: /* REXX exec 9.5 */
"TIME"
"SEND 'SAMPLE EXEC ' USER(*) "
/* this is a sample Exec for REXX class */
Say Time(),
   Date()

Chapter 10

Q 1: What does this program do?
/*REXX TRYME*/
SAY GREETING

A: Displays "GREETING" on the terminal. GREETING is a literal
without quotes.

Q 2: What does this program do?
/*REXX TRY ME TOO*/
GREETING = "HELLO"
SAY GREETING

A: Displays "HELLO"   on the terminal. The literal "HELLO" is put into
the variable GREETING. The contents of the variable GREETING are
displayed on the terminal.

Q 3: Can you tell what this does? (not expected to know).
/*REXX TRY ME TOO*/
GREETING = "HAPPY HALLOWEEN"
SAY GREETING
DROP GREETING
SAY GREETING
Try it at a terminal, if you don't know.

A: Displays "HAPPY HALLOWEEN"   on the terminal, then "GREETING". The literal "HAPPY HALLOWEEN" is put into the variable GREETING. The contents of the variable GREETING are displayed on the terminal. The variable GREETING is undefined, I.E. changed back to a literal without quotes. The literal GREETING is displayed on the terminal.

Q 4: What does this display on the screen?
SAY 'F2F3F4'X

A: 234

Q 5: Write an Exec that displays these lines exactly as shown:

3 + 1 is 4

'3 + 1 is 4'

O'brien

A: /* REXX Exec 12.5 */
Say "3 + 1 is 4"
Say "'3 + 1 is 4'"
Say "O'brien"

Chapter 11

Q 1: What will this display on the terminal?
SAY 5 - 3
A: 2

Q 2: What will this display on the terminal?
SAY "5 - 3"

A: 5 - 3

Q 3: What will this display on the terminal?
SAY "5" - 3

A: 2

Chapter 12

Q 1: Which variable names are invalid and why?
A 1_time_only
B PrOgRaMmEr_nAmE
C prog_name
D input-data
E Say

A: A begins with number
D contains hyphen
E is valid but not recommended

Q 2: What does this exec print out?
/*REXX SHORT EXEC*/
MESSAGE = MESSAGE
SAY MESSAGE
EXIT

A: MESSAGE

Q 3: In an exec, assign the number 10 to a variable. Assign the number 20 to another variable. In one instruction display the total of the two.

A: /* REXX exec 12.3 */
Number1 = 10
Number2 = 20
Say number1 + number2

Chapter 13

Q 1: When this prints out, will there be a blank between Sam and Antha?

SAY "SAM" || "ANTHA"

A: No, because || means string together without blanks.

Q 2: When this prints out, how many blanks will there be between Kelly and Beth?

SAY "KELLY"   "BETH"

A: One. Just putting two things next to each other with one or more blanks, gives ONE blank.

Chapter 14

Q 1: Is 43 = 4.3E1?

A: Yes. 4.3 times 10 to the first power, equals 4.3 times 10.

Q 2: Is 43 = = 4.3E1?

A: No. = = means equal in all respects, not just equivalent.

Q 3: Complete this program segment:

```
/*REXX SAMPLE EXEC*/
NUMBER = 98765
IF NUMBER   12345
THEN

    SAY "THE NUMBER IS 12345"
    END
ELSE
    SAY "I DON'T KNOW WHAT IT IS EQUAL TO"
```

A: ```
/*REXX SAMPLE EXEC*/
NUMBER = 98765
IF NUMBER =   12345
THEN
  DO
   SAY "THE NUMBER IS 12345"
  END
ELSE
  SAY "I DON'T KNOW WHAT IT IS EQUAL TO"
```

Q 4:  Write a program that will:
      Store the number 12 as a constant
      NUMBERA = 12
      Store the number 13 as a constant
      NUMBERB = 13
Then write the instructions that will compare the numbers and find them
equal.

A:    ```
/* REXX exec 14.4 */
NUMBERA = 12
NUMBERB = 13
Numeric digits 2
Numeric Fuzz 1
If NUMBERA = NUMBERB THEN SAY "THEY ARE EQUAL"
```

Q 5: What does this Exec display?
```
A = 5
B = 4
SAY A = B
```

A: 0
    A = B is false, so it becomes a 0.

Q 6: What does this Exec display?
```
A = 2 + 2 = 2
Say A
```

A: 3
    2 = 2   becomes a 1
    2 + 1   = 3

Q 7: Which Boolean operator would you use here?

```
IF YANKEE_MANAGER_A = 'GREEN'                    ,
   YANKEE_MANAGER_B = 'DENT'
THEN SAY 'PLAY BALL'
```

A: You could use | or &&.
    | is either one or the other
    && is just one, not both.

Chapter 15

Q 1: If you execute this Exec with the command shown what are the results?
```
/*REXX Exec runme */
ARG YOUR_NAME ADDRESS            "/" JUNK
SAY "YOUR NAME IS " YOUR_NAME
SAY "YOU LIVE AT  " ADDRESS
= = > RUNME JOHN 22 1/2 MAY ST LIMA PERU
```

A: YOUR NAME IS JOHN
    YOU LIVE AT 22 1
    The info to the right of the / goes into JUNK
    The info to the left of the / goes into YOUR_NAME ADDRESS

Q 2: If you execute this Exec with the command shown what are the results?

```
/*REXX Exec runit*/
ARG  2 YOUR_NAME 5 6 ADDRESS 9
SAY "YOUR NAME IS " YOUR_NAME
SAY "YOU LIVE AT  " ADDRESS
= = > RUNIT JOHN 22 1/2 MAY ST LIMA PERU
```

A: YOUR NAME IS OHN
YOU LIVE AT   22
YOUR_NAME contains columns 2 - 4   ohn
ADDRESS   contains columns 5 - 8   22 1

Q 3: Write an Exec that accepts two ARGS: Day of week, and Weather. If the weather is sunny or cloudy and it's Friday, display Head for Golf Course! But if it's Friday and raining display Head for Office!

A: /* REXX exec 15.3 */
Arg Day_of_week Weather

If (Weather = "SUNNY" | Weather = "CLOUDY"),
  & Day_of_week = "FRIDAY"
Then say "Head for Golf Course"

If Weather = "SUNNY" | Day_of_week = "FRIDAY",
Then say "Head for Office"

Q 4: Write an exec that breaks up the information contained in a variable into three variables. Place this information in the first variable VAR1:

ABCDEFGHIJKLMNOP

Use the proper PARSE instruction to break up the first variable this way:

VAR2 gets columns 3 and 4
VAR3 gets columns 6 through 9
VAR4 gets columns 9 through 14

Display VAR2
Display VAR3
Display VAR4

Expected Results:

CD
FGHI
IJKLMN

A: /* REXX problem 15.4 */
VAR1 = "ABCDEFGHIJKLMNOP"
PARSE VAR VAR1 3 VAR2 5 6 VAR4 10 9 VAR3 14
SAY VAR2
SAY VAR3
SAY VAR4

Chapter 16

Q 1: What would this say?
/*REXX sample 16.1*/
ARG N1 N2 N3
SAY N2 N3 N1

If it is executed this way?
= = > TESTING MARYELLEN SUE KAREN

A: SUE KAREN MARYELLEN

Q 2: Write an exec that will execute this TSO command:
LISTCAT ENTRY(dataset-name)
The dataset name is to be entered thru an ARG. Make sure it works on
datsets belonging to you as well as those belonging to someone else.
Try executing it with these two dataset names:
REXXPRGS.EXEC
'SYS1.PROCLIB'

A: /* REXX exec 16.2 */
ARG Dataset_name
"LISTCAT ENTRY("Dataset_name")"

= = > %myexec REXXPRGS.EXEC
= = > %myexec 'SYS1.PROCLIB'

Q 3: This ARG, and this manner of execution produces what display?

/*REXX addemup exec*/
ARG NUM1 NUM2 NUM3 .
TOTAL = NUM1 + NUM2 + NUM3
SAY TOTAL

= = = > ADDEMUP 10 20 30 40 50 60

A: 60
40 50 60 are thrown away

Q 4: Write an Exec that accepts three pieces of information and displays them in reverse order. If more than 3 entered, display an error message.

A: ```
/*REXX 16.4   */
ARG A B C D
IF D <> ''
THEN SAY "I said enter only three items please!"
SAY C B A
```

Q 5: Write an Exec that examines information typed in when it is executed.
    If both "Mike" and "George" are typed in, display
        "incompatible attributes"
    If only "Mike" typed in, display
        "are you a Democrat?"
    If only "George" typed in, display
        "are you a Republican?"
    If neither one is typed in, display an error message
    Expected Results:
    = = = > %myexec mike george
        INCOMPATIBLE ATTRIBUTES
    = = = > %myexec mike
        ARE YOU A DEMOCRAT?
    = = = > %myexec george
        ARE YOU A REPUBLICAN?
    = = = > %myexec curly moe
        PLEASE ENTER THE RIGHT NAMES

A:  ```
/*REXX gallup poll*/
ARG NAME1 NAME2 .
IF  NAME1 = "MIKE" & NAME2 = "GEORGE"
THEN SAY "INCOMPATIBLE ATTRIBUTES"
IF  NAME2 = "MIKE" & NAME1 = "GEORGE"
THEN SAY "INCOMPATIBLE ATTRIBUTES"
IF  NAME1 = "MIKE" | NAME2 = "MIKE"
THEN SAY "ARE YOU A DEMOCRAT?    "
IF  NAME1 = "GEORGE" | NAME2 = "GEORGE"
THEN SAY "ARE YOU A REPUBLICAN?  "
IF NAME1 <> "GEORGE" & NAME1 <> "MIKE" &,
NAME2 <> "GEORGE" & NAME2 <> "MIKE"
THEN SAY "PLEASE ENTER THE RIGHT NAMES"
```

Another way:

```
ARG MIKE GEORGE
IF MIKE = 'GEORGE'
THEN
  DO
   HOLD_GEORGE = GEORGE
   GEORGE = MIKE
   MIKE = HOLD_GEORGE
  END
IF GEORGE = 'MIKE'
THEN
  DO
   HOLD_MIKE = MIKE
   MIKE = GEORGE
   GEORGE = HOLD_MIKE
  END
IF MIKE = "MIKE" & GEORGE = "GEORGE"
THEN SAY "INCOMPATIBLE ATTRIBUTES"
IF MIKE = "MIKE" & GEORGE <> "GEORGE"
THEN SAY "ARE YOU A DEMOCRAT"
IF GEORGE = "GEORGE" & MIKE <> "MIKE"
THEN SAY "ARE YOU A REPUBLICAN"
IF MIKE <> "MIKE" & GEORGE <> "GEORGE"
THEN SAY "PLEASE ENTER THE RIGHT NAMES"
```

Chapter 17

Q 1: You want the user to type in 3 and only 3 items (words) of information, separated by spaces. What does your PULL look like?

A: PULL V1 V2 V3 .

Q 2: Write an Exec that asks for 3 words (only) and displays them in reverse order.

A:
```
/*REXX Exec myexec */
SAY "PLEASE ENTER 3 WORDS (ONLY)"
PULL W1 W2 W3 .
SAY W3 W2 W1
```

Q 3: Write a front end exec for the DELETE command. Have it ask "are you sure?" If the data set name is "junk.data" don't ask.

> Expected results:
> = = = > %erase abc.data
>   ARE YOU SURE? Y/N
> = = = > n
>   NOT DELETED
> = = = > %erase junk.data
>   DELETED

A: /* REXX SAMPLE 17.3*/
ARG DATASET
IF DATASET = "JUNK.DATA"
THEN "DELETE " DATASET
ELSE
  DO
    SAY "ARE YOU SURE? Y/N "
    PULL REPLY
    IF REPLY = "Y" THEN "DELETE " DATASET
    ELSE SAY "NOT DELETED"
  END

Q 4: Write an Exec that computes the percent of increase of one number over another. Ask for the two amounts from the terminal.

> The formula is:
>   % increase = 100 * ((new - old) / old)

> Imagine your old salary was 21,203 and your new is 80,000.
> You would figure the % increase as
>   % increase = 100 * ((80000 - 21203) / 21203)

> Expected results:
> = = = > %myexec 100 120
>   20

A: /* REXX exec 17.4 */
Say "Please enter your old salary "
Pull Old
Say "Please enter your new salary "
Pull New
Percent_increase = 100 * ((New - Old) / Old)
Say "% increase is " Percent_increase

Q 5: Ask for the weather from the terminal, and the day of the week.
If it's raining, ask how many inches.
If it's Friday and sunny, or cloudy
display "head for golf course".
If it's Saturday and less than .5 inches,
display "fishing pole please".

A: /* REXX exec 17.5 */
Say "What is the weather?"
Pull Weather
Say "What is the day of week?"
Pull Day_of_week
If Weather = "RAINING"
  then
      do
      Say "How many inches of rain?"
      Pull Inches
      end

If Day_of_week = "FRIDAY" ,
& (Weather = "SUNNY" | Weather = "CLOUDY")
then Say "Head for golf course"

If Day_of_week = "SATURDAY" & inches < .5
then Say "Fish pole please"

Chapter 18

Q 1: Your program is running, apparently not doing anything, and won't
stop. What do you type in to see what it is doing?

A: Press PA1, then type in TS. That turns on interactive trace, then you
can single-step thru your program by hitting ENTER.

Q 2: You are in interactive trace, single stepping through the program.
You've had enough. What do you type in to make the program run without
any trace?

A: TRACE ?N
     or
     TRACE OFF
     or
     "EXECUTIL TE   "
     then hit ENTER once again.

Q 3: Can you regain control of your runaway Exec by typing in "EXECUTIL TS "?

A: No
Press PA1 or ATTN first, then TS will stop your exec, while it is running, and out of your control.

Q 4: Can you put "EXECUTIL TS in your Exec as an instruction, to turn on interactive debug?

A: Yes. It is a TSO command, and can be used in an exec.

Chapter 19

Q 1: Should you leave ERROR traps in Execs that go into production?

A: Yes. A command to the environment may fail later, after working for a time. You can put out an error message, and stop any further damage.

Q 2: Does the NOVALUE trap help to enforce a good programming practice?

A: Yes. You should always distinguish between variables and literals.

Q 3: ERRORTEXT(RC) is used in which error trap?

A: The REXX syntax error trap. It's not used in environment command error traps.

Q 4: Complete this Exec
```
/*REXX sample *
SIGNAL ON ERROR
SIGNAL ON
"TURN DOWN VOLUME"
SAY 1 * ( 2 + 3 (
EXIT

SAY "COMMAND TO TSO FAILED"

SYNTAX:
   SAY "SYNTAX ERROR ON LINE "
   EXIT
```

A: /*REXX sample*/
    SIGNAL ON ERROR
    SIGNAL ON SYNTAX
    "TURN DOWN VOLUME"
    SAY 1 * (2 + 3 (
    EXIT
    ERROR:
        SAY "COMMAND TO TSO FAILED"
        EXIT
    SYNTAX:
        SAY "SYNTAX ERROR ON LINE " SIGL
        EXIT

Q 5: Write an exec that asks for a dataset name and then issues the TSO command LISTD on it. Set up an error trap to intercept the command not working. In the error trap, display the line of the program in error, the error code from TSO. Ask for the dataset name again, reexecute the command and exit.

    Expected results:
    = = = > %myexec
        PLEASE ENTER DATASET NAME
    = = = > abc.nonesuch.data
        CANNOT EXECUTE TSO COMMAND
        TSO ERROR CODE IS 12
        LINE IN ERROR IS "LISTDS" DSN
        PLEASE REENTER
    = = = > abc.real.data
        ABC.REAL.DATA VOLUME SERIAL D12345
        LRECL 80 BLKSIZE 3120 RECFM FB

A: /* REXX exec 19.5 */
    SIGNAL ON ERROR
    SAY "PLEASE ENTER DATASET NAME "
    PULL DSN
    "LISTDS " DSN
    EXIT

    ERROR:
        SAY "CANNOT EXECUTE TSO COMMAND"
        SAY "TSO ERROR CODE IS " RC
        SAY "LINE IN ERROR IS " SOURCELINE(SIGL)
        SAY "PLEASE REENTER"
        PULL DSN
        "LISTDS " DSN
        EXIT

Chapter 20

Q 1: Write an Exec that will multiply two numbers, prompt the user for the two numbers, set up an error trap to intercept any error, such as invalid numbers.

A: /*REXX EXEC MULTIPLY */
     SAY "PLEASE ENTER TWO NUMBERS"
     PULL NUMBER1 NUMBER2
     SIGNAL ON SYNTAX
     SAY NUMBER1 * NUMBER
     EXIT
     SYNTAX: SAY "SOMETHING WRONG WITH YOUR NUMBERS"

     EXIT

Q 2:   Run this Exec to determine the effect of parentheses on arithmetic operations.

     SAY (1 + 2) * 3
     SAY 1 + (2 * 3)
     SAY 1 + 2 * 3
What is displayed?

A: 9
     7
     7

Q 3: Write an Exec that asks for a number (record length) and another number (block size). It determines if block size is an exact multiple of record length, I.E. if record length was multiplied by a whole number to obtain block size.
     Expected results:
     = = = > %myexec
          PLEASE ENTER RECORD LENGTH
     = = = > 80
          PLEASE ENTER BLOCK SIZE
     = = = > 3121
          BLOCK SIZE IS NOT A MULTIPLE OF RECORD LENGTH

```
A:   /*REXX exec 20.3 */
     SAY "ENTER RECORD LENGTH, BLOCK SIZE"
     PULL REC_L BLOCK_SIZE
     IF BLOCK_SIZE // REC_L = 0
     THEN EXIT
        SAY "NOT A MULTIPLE"
```

Chapter 21

Q 1: Correct this segment of code.
```
/*REXX sample with errors */
CASE
   WHEN "NAME" = "JOHN" THEN SAY "GRADE IS 78"
   WHEN  NAME  = "MARY" THEN SAY "GRADE IS 84"
   WHEN  NAME  = "MIKE" THEN SAY "GRADE IS 89"
   WHEN  NAME  = "MONA" THEN SAY "GRADE IS 91"
ELSE  THEN SAY "NOT ON ROSTER"
```

A:
```
/*REXX sample without errors*/
SELECT
   WHEN  NAME  = "JOHN" THEN SAY "GRADE IS 78"
   WHEN  NAME  = "MARY" THEN SAY "GRADE IS 84"
   WHEN  NAME  = "MIKE" THEN SAY "GRADE IS 89"
   WHEN  NAME  = "MONA" THEN SAY "GRADE IS 91"
OTHERWISE  SAY "NOT ON ROSTER"
END
```

Q 2: Are these two segments of code equivalent?
```
/*sample1        */
SELECT
   WHEN  NAME  = "ERIC" THEN SAY "GRADE IS 83"
OTHERWISE  SAY "NOT ON ROSTER"
END

/*sample2 */
IF NAME = "ERIC"
THEN SAY "GRADE IS 83"
ELSE SAY "NOT ON ROSTER"
```

A: Yes

Chapter 22

Q 1: Will this line of instruction be passed to the environment?

Pull var1 var2 var3

A: No. REXX understands the keyword Pull.

Q 2: Will this line of instruction be passed to the environment?

ARTICULATE "PLEASE ENTER NAME "

A: Yes. REXX doesn't understand ARTICULATE.

Q 3: If this command works, what will be in RC?

"DELETE ABC.DATA"

A: 0

Q 4: Can you always talk to ISPF from any Exec?

A: No. ISPF is present only if you are executing your Exec from within ISPF.

Q 5: Write an Exec to copy your setup exec (any dataset will do) to the dataset: TEMP.COPY.DATA.
Pass this command to TSO:
COPY REXXPRGS.EXEC(SETUP) TEMP.COPY.DATA NONUM

(The NONUM operand needed to assure a true copy). If the return code is zero, then issue the TSO command LIST TEMP.COPY.DATA.
Note: Both commands are optional program products. Your installation may not have them.

A:
```
/* REXX exec 22.5 */
"COPYREXXPRGS.EXEC(SETUP)TEMP.COPY.DATANONUM"

IF RC = 0
Then
  Do
   "LIST TEMP.COPY.DATA"
  End
```

Q 6: See if ISPF is available. If so, then browse your setup exec.
The command to do that is:
BROWSE DATASET(the-dataset)
Pass it to the ISPEXEC environment.

If not, use the TSO command LIST to view it.
The command to do that is:
LIST dataset
To test it, execute it once inside of ISPF, once outside.

A: /* REXX sample 22.6 */
"SUBCOM" "ISPEXEC"
IF RC = 0
THEN ADDRESS "ISPEXEC" "BROWSE DATASET(REXXPRGS.EXEC)"
ELSE "LIST REXXPRGS.EXEC(SETUP)"

Q 7:   Is the environment ISPEXEC always available?

A: No. ISPF is present only if you are executing your Exec from within
ISPF. ISPEXEC is the name of the ISPF environment.

Chapter 23

Q 1:   There must be a space after the name of the function, and before the
parenthesis when you use the function. Yes/No.

A: No. there must be no space. function-name(data)

Q 2:   When you call a built-in function with CALL where is the answer
given?

A: In the special variable RESULT.

Q 3:   Accept 2 numbers from the terminal. Check to be sure they are valid
numbers. Subtract one from the other. Drop the sign of the answer, display
the answer.

Expected results:
= = = > %myexec 100 20
80
= = = > %myexec 20 100
80

A: /*REXX 23.3*/
ARG NUM1 NUM2 .
IF DATATYPE(NUM1) < > "NUM"
THEN DO
    SAY "FIRST NUMBER INVALID"
    END
IF DATATYPE(NUM2) < > "NUM"
THEN DO
    SAY "SECOND NUMBER INVALID"
    END
SAY ABS(NUM1 - NUM2)

Q 4:   Use SYSDSN to see if there exists a dataset named WORKSHOP.TEMP. If so, delete it. If not, allocate a new one like your Exec library.
The TSO command is:
    ALLOC DSN(WORKSHOP.TEMP) LIKE(REXXPRGS.EXEC)

A: /* REXX Sample 23.4   */
If Sysdsn("WORKSHOP.TEMP") = "OK"
then
    do
    "DELETE WORKSHOP.TEMP"
    end
else
    do
    "ALLOC DSN(WORKSHOP.TEMP) LIKE(REXXPRGS.EXEC)"

    end

Q 5:   Redo the previous one, supressing any display message from the DELETE command, by using OUTTRAP.

A: /* REXX Sample 23.6   */
If Sysdsn("WORKSHOP.TEMP") = "OK"
then
    do
    Dummy = Outtrap("dummy2",0)
    "DELETE WORKSHOP.TEMP"
    Dummy = Outtrap("OFF")
    end
else
    do
    "ALLOC DSN(WORKSHOP.TEMP) LIKE(REXXPRGS.EXEC)"
    end

Q 6:   Redo the previous one, supressing any display message from the
DELETE command, by using the MSG function.

A: /* REXX Sample 23.6   */
```
If Sysdsn("WORKSHOP.TEMP") = "OK"
then
    do
    Dummy = Msg("OFF")
    "DELETE WORKSHOP.TEMP"
    Dummy = Msg("ON")
    end
else
    do
    "ALLOCDSN(WORKSHOP.TEMP)LIKE(REXXPRGS.EXEC)"

    end
```

Q 7: Using a function, create an exec that will convert one character string
to another. Set it up so that if you type in:

          ES BUENO
it will print out:
          IT'S NICE

A: /*REXX 23.7 */

```
String = "IT'S NICE"
SAY TRANSLATE(STRING,"NOE SU B","CEISTN'")
```

Q 8: Write an exec that will accept a hex number, a plus or minus sign, and
another hex number, then add or subtract based on the sign. Display the
answer in hex.

      Expected results:
      = = = > %hexmath e - 2
          C
      = = = > %hexmath e + 2
          10

A: `/* REXX 23.8 */`
        `Arg Hex1 Sign Hex2`
        `Ans = 0`
        `Dec1 = x2d(Hex1)`
        `Dec2 = x2d(Hex2)`
        `If Sign = "+"`
        `Then Ans = Dec1 + Dec2`
          `If Sign = "-"`
          `Then Ans = Dec1 - Dec1`
        `Say D2x(Ans)`

Chapter 24

Q 1: In REXX, user-written functions/subroutines may be used either as functions or subroutines. Yes/No.

A: Yes

Q 2: If you use it as a function, you do it this way:
              function-name(data)   T/F.

A: T

Q 3: If you use it as a subroutine, you do it this way:
              CALL function-name data
and the answer comes back in RESULT. T/F.

A: T

Q 4: Write an internal function/subroutine that will concatenate two items passed to it (without spaces). Invoke it both ways. Check automatically within the Exec that both ways produce the same result.

A: `/*REXX Exec testit*/`
        `CALL CONCAT "CAT","DOG"`
        `SAVE_RESULT = RESULT`
        `IF SAVE_RESULT = = CONCAT("CAT","DOG)`
        `THEN SAY "RESULTS ARE EQUAL"`
        `ELSE SAY "RESULTS NOT EQUAL"`
        `EXIT`
        `CONCAT: PROCEDURE`
          `ARG A,B`
          `RETURN A || B`

Q 5: Redo the % increase problem as an external subroutine. Name it PERCENTI (see problem 17.4). Have it accept two parameters (I.E. arguments). First: Old salary, Second: New salary. Have it return the % increase on the RETURN statement. Check both numbers for numeric. If either is not valid, display a message and return a zero. Write another exec to test this one, by calling it as a function, then as a subroutine. Place both in the same Exec library.

A:
```
/* REXX external subroutine/function that
   calculates percent of increase */
ARG Old_salary  New_salary
If datatype(Old_salary) = "NUM",
&   datatype(Old_salary) = "NUM"
then nop
  else
    do
      Say "Number is invalid"
      Return 0
    end

Return 100 * ((New_salary - Old_salary) / old_salary)

/* REXX Main exec to test %increase subroutine 24.5*/
Say "PERCENTI"(20000 , 22000 )

Call "PERCENTI" 20000 , 22000
Say Result
```

Q 6: Using solution to Problem 24.4, write your concatenate function/subroutine as an external function/subroutine (leave the internal where it is). Call the external function/subroutine in such a way that you are sure to invoke the external not the internal. Prove that you invoked the external, not the internal.

A:
```
/*REXX Exec testit*/
CALL "CONCAT" "CAT","DOG"
SAVE_RESULT = RESULT
IF SAVE_RESULT = = "CONCAT"("CAT","DOG)
THEN SAY "RESULTS ARE EQUAL"
ELSE SAY "RESULTS NOT EQUAL"
EXIT
CONCAT: PROCEDURE /*INTERNAL*/
        ARG A,B
        SAY "IM IN THE INTERNAL"
        RETURN A || B
```

```
/*REXX Exec Concat EXTERNAL*/
ARG A,B
SAY "IM IN THE EXTERNAL"
RETURN A || B
```

Q 7: Create a Metric conversion external subroutine/function named Metric. It will accept two arguments: UNIT and QUANTITY. UNIT has these possible values:

LITER   QUART   MILE   KILOMETER

It returns a number which is the equivalent of QUANTITY, in the other measuring system, based upon this table:

```
1 liter     = 1.057 quarts
1 quart     = .946  liters
1 mile      = 8/5   kilometers
1 kilometer = .625  miles
```

Also write a main Exec that invokes this as a function.

Expected results:
```
= = = > %myexec kilometer 1000
        625 MILES
```

A:
```
/* REXX external subr METRIC */
ARG UNIT , QUANTITY
IF UNIT = "LITER" THEN ANSWER = QUANTITY * 1.057
IF UNIT = "QUART" THEN ANSWER = QUANTITY * .946
IF UNIT = "MILE"  THEN ANSWER = QUANTITY * (8/5)
IF UNIT = "KILOMETER" THEN ANSWER = QUANTITY * .625
RETURN ANSWER

/*REXX MAIN PROGRAM */
SAY "10 MILES IS " "METRIC"("MILE",10) "KM"
/*ANOTHER WAY*/
CALL "METRIC" "MILE",10
SAY "10 MILES IS " RESULT "KM"
```

Chapter 25

Q 1: Can the Concat function/subroutine that you did be done as a separate program?

A: No, because a program can pass back only a number. This passes back a character string.

Chapter 26

Q 1: What is the missing word?

```
DO FOREVER
    SAY "WHAT NUMBER AM I THINKING OF. 1-10"
    PULL NUMBER
    IF NUMBER = 7
        THEN
        SAY "STILL HAVEN'T GOT IT"
END
SAY "GOOD GUESS. GOING TO TRY THE LOTTERY NEXT?"
```

A:
```
DO FOREVER
    SAY "WHAT NUMBER AM I THINKING OF. 1-10"
    PULL NUMBER
    IF NUMBER = 7
        THEN  LEAVE
    SAY "STILL HAVEN'T GOT IT"
END
SAY "GOOD GUESS. GOING TO TRY THE LOTTERY NEXT?"
```

Q 2: Write an Exec that asks the user to enter a series of numbers, but never enter the same one twice in a row. Limit it to 10 numbers.

A:
```
DO 10
    SAY "ENTER A NUMBER (DIFFERENT FROM LAST ONE)"
    PULL NUMBER
    IF NUMBER = PREVIOUS_NUMBER
    THEN  SAY "SAME AS LAST ONE!"
    PREVIOUS_NUMBER = NUMBER
END
```

Q 3: Write an external subroutine to compute the square root of a number passed to it. Name it SQRT. It will accept one ARG: the number. Validate the number. If negative, or not numeric, display a message, return a zero. Establish a tolerance of .01 for determining when to exit the loop. Establish a loop limit of 50, as maximum times to do the loop. Make your guess 1/2 of the number.

Repeat this loop loop_limit times
    Make new guess = (guess + (number / guess)) / 2
    If the difference between new guess and guess
    is less than the tolerance,
    exit the loop.
    Make guess = new guess
end-repeat
Return the new guess to the caller.

A:
```
/* REXX function/subroutine to calculate square root
    negative numbers not allowed */
ARG Number
/* Validate Number */
If datatype(Number) < > "NUM"
then
   do
     Say "Argument passed not a number "
     Return 0
   end
If Number < 0
then
   do
     Say "Cannot process negative numbers"
     Return 0
   end
/* Initialize Variables */
Tolerance = .01
Loop_limit = 50
Guess = Number / 2
/* Keep guessing till guess is close /*
Do I = 1 to Loop_limit
     New_guess = (Guess + (Number / Guess)) / 2
     If Abs(New_guess - Guess) < Tolerance then leave
     Guess = New_guess
     /* For debugging say New_guess */
End
/* For debugging, say New_guess * New_guess */
Return New_guess
```

```
/* REXX exec to test square root function/subrout*/
Say "SQRT"(144)
Say "SQRT"(-144)
Call "SQRT" 144
Say RESULT
```

Q 4: Set secret-number equal to 13. Write an exec to keep asking the user to enter a number from 1 to 20 until the secret-number is guessed. Limit the loop to 10 guesses.

Expected results:
```
= = > %myexec
    PLEASE ENTER YOUR GUESS, FROM 1 TO 20
= = > 2
    WRONG
= = > 7
    WRONG
= = > 13
    RIGHT
```

A: ```
/* REXX 26.4 */
Secret_number = 13
Guess = ""
Do 10
   Say "Please enter your guess, from 1 to 20"
   Pull guess
   If Guess = secret_number
   Then
     Do
       Say "RIGHT"
       LEAVE
     End
   Else
     Do
       Say "WRONG"
     End
End /* Do 10 */
```

## Chapter 27

Q 1:  What will this line of a REXX program do?
```
SAY QUEUED()
```

A:  It will display how many lines are in the program stack
```

Q 2: There is nothing in the stack. Your program says PULL. What happens?

A: Keyboard unlocks.

Q 3: Your Exec does 10 PUSHes, and 9 PULLs. What happens?

A: Error message from TSO.

Q 4: Your Exec does 9 PUSHes, and 10 PULLs. What happens?

A: Keyboard unlocks.

Q 5: Accept a dataset name from the terminal. Verify that the dataset name is less than 45 characters long. Verify that it exists. Place the dataset name into the Stack, so the LISTDS command can get it. Suggestion: place it LIFO. Use PUSH command.

Turn on prompting. Execute the TSO command LISTDS, but omit the dataset name, this makes TSO prompt you for it, but it's in the Stack, and LISTDS gets it from there.

A:
```
/* REXX sample 27.5 */
ARG Dataset_name
If Length(Dataset_name) > 44
Then
  do
    Say "Dataset name was too long "
    Say "Terminating"
    Exit
  end
If Sysdsn(Dataset_name) = "OK"
Then
  do
    Nop
  end
Else
  do
    Say "Dataset name doesn't exist"
    Say "Terminating"
    Exit
  end

"PROFILE PROMPT"
Hold_prompt = Prompt("ON")
PUSH Dataset_name
"LISTDS"
```

Chapter 28

Q 1: Write an Exec with a loop that sets NUMBER.1 thru NUMBER.10 to the numbers 101 thru 110, then loop through the array, displaying the contents of NUMBER.1 thru NUMBER.11. Yes, NUMBER.11, to see what happens.

```
A:   DO I = 1 TO 10
       NUMBER.I = I + 100
     END
     DO I = 1 TO 11
       SAY NUMBER.I
     END
```

Q 2: Write a capture exec, that captures the display from TSO commands, in an array, then displays the lines of output one at a time. Display "Please enter a command". Accept the command, into a variable. Turn on Outtrap, using the array Display_line. Turn off Outtrap. Display the message: "About to display command's output". Loop thru the array, displaying each line of the command's output.

```
A:   /* REXX sample 28.2 */
     Say "Please enter a TSO command"
     Pull TSO_command
     Dummy = Outtrap("Display_line.","*")
     TSO_command

     Dummy = Outtrap("OFF")
     Say "About to display command's output"
     Do I = 1 to Display_line.0
       Say Display_line.I
     End
```

Chapter 29

Q 1: If the EXECIO command works properly, the variable RC is set to what?

A: 0

Chapter 32

Q 1: Choose a file that you currently have under your userid. Read it into an array. Display every other record, starting with record 1.

A:
```
/* REXX sample 32.1 */
"ALLOC DSN(ANYNAME.DATA) SHR REUSE DDN(INFILE)"

"EXECIO * DISKR INFILE  (STEM RECD."
DO I = 1 TO RECD.0 BY 2
   SAY RECD.I
END
```

Q 2: Read in a file that you currently have under your userid. Read it into an array. Write it out to another file. Get both file names from the terminal by asking. To allocate the new file, use an allocate command with LIKE.

A:
```
/* REXX sample 32.2 */
Say "Please enter 'from' dataset name"
Pull From_name
Say "Please enter 'to'  dataset name"
Pull  To_name
"ALLOCATE DDNAME(INFILE   SHR DSNAME("From_name")"
"ALLOCATE DDNAME(OUTFILE) NEW DSNAME("To_name ")",
 " LIKE(TEST.DATA)"
"EXECIO *       DISKR INFILE  (STEM RECORD. FINIS"
"EXECIO"RECORD.0 "DISKW OUTFILE (STEM RECORD. FINIS"
"FREE DDNAME(OUTFILE)"
"FREE DDNAME(INFILE) "
```

Q 3: Read any file of yours into an array 1 record at a time. As you read, count each record. Keep track of the length of the longest record. At the end of the program, display the record count, and the length of the longest record.

A:
```
/* REXX sample 32.3 */
Max_length = 0

"ALLOC DSN(ANYNAME.DATA) SHR REUSE DDN(INFILE)"
"EXECIO * DISKR INFILE (STEM RECD. FINIS"
DO I = 1 TO RECD.0
   IF LENGTH(RECD.I) > MAX_LENGTH
   THEN MAX_LENGTH = LENGTH(RECD.I)
END
SAY "RECORD COUNT " RECD.0
SAY "LONGEST RECORD WAS " MAX_LENGTH
```

Q 4: Modify the CAPTURE exec (Problem 28.1) to store the lines of the display in the dataset
   TEMP.CAPTURE.DATA
Use SYSDSN to see if that dataset exists. If it exists, delete it. Then allocate it (create it), with the following TSO command:

   ALLOC DSN(TEMP.CAPTURE.DATA) DDNAME(CAPTURE)
   SPACE(1 1) TRACKS LRECL(80) BLOCK(4000) RECFM(F B)
   (Normally typed in on one line, not two).

Outtrap loads an array. Use that array to write out the lines of the command display. The Write command should close the file at the same time.

```
A:   /* REXX sample 32.4 */
     Say "Please enter a TSO command"
     Pull TSO_command
     Dummy = Outtrap("LINE.","*")
     TSO_command
     Dummy = Outtrap("OFF")
     IF SYSDSN("TEMP.CAPTURE.DATA") = "OK"
     THEN
   "ALLOC DSN(TEMP.CAPTURE.DATA) SHR DDNAME(CAPTURE)"
     ELSE
       DO
       "ALLOC DSN(TEMP.CAPTURE.DATA) DDNAME(CAPTURE)",
       "SPACE(1 1) TRACKS LRECL(80) BLOCK(4000) RECFM(FB)"
       END
     "EXECIO " LINE.0 "DISKW CAPTURE (STEM LINE. FINIS "
```

Chapter 33

Q 1: Create a quick calculator exec. Use INTERPRET to execute an expression that is typed in. Display the result. Name it CALC. It will be used this way:
   = = > %CALC 1 + 1
   It will display 2

```
A:   /* REXX CALC exec */
     ARG Expression
     Signal.on syntax
     Interpret "Say " Expression
     Exit
     Syntax:
     Say "Syntax error in expression " Expresion
     Exit
```

Q 1: Write an ISPF Editor macro to save and execute the Exec that you are editing. Name it Runit. It must start off with the usual comment then
ADDRESS "ISREDIT" "MACRO PROCESS"
Pass this command to the ISPF Editor:
REPLACE TESTXXXX .ZF .ZL
Pass this command to TSO:
EXEC your-exec-library(TESTXXXX) EXEC
It will work with libraries only. To execute it, type RUNIT on the command line in the editor.

A: /* REXX exec 34.1*/
ADDRESS "ISREDIT" "MACRO PROCESS"
ADDRESS "ISREDIT" "REPLACE TESTXXXX .ZF .ZL"
"EXEC REXXPRGS(TESTXXXX) EXEC "

/* REXX exec 34.1a how it's done with parms*/
ADDRESS "ISREDIT" "MACRO (PARM1,PARM2) PROCESS"
ADDRESS "ISREDIT" "REPLACE TESTXXXX .ZF .ZL"
"EXEC REXXPRGS(TESTXXXX) " 'PARM1 PARM2' " EXEC"

Q 2: Enhance problem 34.1. Check to see if you are trying to execute RUNIT. Get the member name from the editor. If the member name is RUNIT, issue message, exit.

A: /* REXX exec 34.1*/
ADDRESS "ISREDIT" "MACRO   PROCESS"
ADDRESS "ISREDIT" "(MEMBR) = MEMBER"
IF MEMBR = "RUNIT"
THEN
   DO
    SAY "CANNOT USE RUNIT TO EXECUTE RUNIT"
    EXIT
   END
ADDRESS "ISREDIT" "REPLACE TESTXXXX .ZF .ZL"
"EXEC REXXPRGS(TESTXXXX) EXEC "

Appendix B

FUNCTIONS. FULL LIST

All functions listed in this Appendix are supported under both TSO and CMS, unless marked "TSO", or "CMS".

ABBREV

ABBREV(*word,abbrev,length*)

Is *abbrev* a valid abbreviation of *word* , considering *length* characters, of *word*?

        YES ---> 1
        NO ---> 0

                SAY ABBREV('ALLOCATE','ALEXANDER',2)
                ---> 1

ABS

ABS(*number*)

Drop the sign of *number*. Format result according to current NUMERIC settings.

                SAY ABS(-123.45)
                ---> 123.45

ADDRESS

ADDRESS()

Return the current environment that commands are being sent to.

```
--- > TSO        {
--- > MVS        {  under TSO
--- > ISPEXEC      {

--- > CMS        {
--- > COMMAND      {  under CMS
--- > XEDIT       {
```

```
SAY ADDRESS()
--- > TSO
--- > COMMAND
```

ARG

ARG()

How many argument strings were passed? (Commas delimit argument strings). You can pass several to a Function/Subroutine, only one to a main program.

```
--- > 0
--- > 1
--- > etc
```

```
= = = > CALL MYEXEC SALLY, KAREN SUSAN
SAY ARG()
--- > 2
```

ARG(*number*)

If *number* is a 1, return the first argument string. If *number* is a 2, return the second argument string, etc.

> = = = > CALL MYEXEC SALLY, KAREN SUSAN
> SAY ARG(2)
> ---> KAREN SUSAN

CENTER

CENTER(*string,length,pad*)

Centers *string* within a larger string of *length*. *Pad*, if present, is the pad character instead of spaces.

> SAY CENTER('MIDDLE',14)
> --->   MIDDLE

> SAY CENTER('MIDDLE',14.'-')
> ---> ----MIDDLE---

COMPARE

COMPARE(*string1,string2,pad*)

Compares *string1* to *string2*. *Pad*, if present, is the pad character instead of spaces. If both strings equal, returns a 0, otherwise returns the character position of inequality.

> SAY COMPARE('APPLES','APPLES')
> ---> 0

> SAY COMPARE('APPLES','APPLESAUCE')
> ---> 7

CONDITION TSO Only.

CONDITION('D')

Returns the string in error within a Condition trap.

SAY CONDITION('D')
---> "ABC" - "DEF"

COPIES

COPIES(*string,how many*)

Returns *how many* copies of *string*, side by side.

SAY COPIES('DO',2)
---> DODO

C2D

C2D(*string*)

Convert *string* to a binary representation, then to decimal value.

SAY C2D('a')
---> 129

SAY C2D('81'X)
---> 129

C2X

C2X(*string*)

Convert *string* to a 'hexadecimal' representation.

SAY C2X('A123')
---> C1F1F2F3

DATATYPE

DATATYPE(*string*)

Returns NUM if *string* is a valid number, otherwise CHAR.

```
---> NUM
---> CHAR
        SAY DATATYPE(1234)
        ---> NUM
        SAY DATATYPE(X234)
        ---> CHAR
```

DATATYPE

DATATYPE(*string,type*)

Returns 1 if *string* corresponds to *type*, otherwise 0.

```
types:
        A - alphanumeric A-Z, a-z, 0-9
        B - binary digits 1 and 0
        D - double byte character set
        L - lowercase letters
        M - mixed case
        N - valid number
        L - lowercase letters
        S - symbol: valid REXX symbol
        U - uppercase letters
        W - whole number
        X - hexadecimal number    0-9 or A-F
---> 1
---> 0
```

```
        SAY DATATYPE(A234,N)
        ---> 0
        SAY DATATYPE(A234,A)
        ---> 1
```

DATE

DATE()

Returns current date in format 25 Dec 1989.

---> 25 Dec 1989

        SAY DATE()
        ---> 25 Dec 1991

DATE

DATE(*type*)

Returns date corrresponding to *type*.

>   *types:*
>   B - basedate: number of complete days since
>   Jan 1, year 1.
>   C - century: number of days in this century to now.
>   D - days: number of days so far this year.
>   E - European date: format dd/mm/yy
>   J - Julian date: format yyddd
>   M - Name of current month
>   O - Ordered: date suitable for sorting: yy/mm/dd
>   S - Sorting: date suitable for sorting: yyyy/mm/dd
>   U - USA format: mm/dd/yy
>   W - Name of current weekday

DELSTR

DELSTR(*string,start char,length*)

Deletes characters from *string* beginning at *start char*, for a length of *length*.

        SAY DELSTR('ABCDEF',2,3)
        ---> AEF

DELWORD

DELWORD(*string,start word,how many words*)

Deletes *how many words* words from *string*, beginning with *start word*.

SAY DELWORD('Mary had a little lamb',2,3)
---> Mary lamb

DIAGRC CMS only.

DIAGRC(*code,"command to CP"*)

Passes *code* to CP, and the *command to CP*. Reply from CP is the result of the function. RC contains a return code from CP.

SAY DIAGRC(8,"QUERY READER")
---> NO FILES IN READER

DIGITS

DIGITS()

Returns the current setting of NUMERIC DIGITS.

NUMERIC DIGITS 7
SAY DIGITS()
---> 7

D2C

D2C(*number*)

Converts a decimal *number* to a binary value. The inverse of C2D.

SAY D2C(129)
---> a   (internally represented as 81)

D2X

D2X(*number*)

Converts a decimal *number* to a hexadecimal value. The inverse of X2D.

> SAY D2X(129)
> ---> 81

ERRORTEXT

ERRORTEXT(*number*)

Returns the REXX syntax error message corresponding to *number*.

> SAY ERRORTEXT(16)
> ---> LABEL NOT FOUND

EXTERNALS

EXTERNALS()

In TSO/REXX, always returns a 0.
In VM/REXX, returns the number of elements in the terminal input buffer.

> SAY EXTERNALS()
> ---> 0

FIND

FIND(*string,phrase*)

Returns the word number of the first word of *phrase* in *string*.

> SAY FIND('MARY HAD A LITTLE LAMB','A LITTLE LAMB')
> ---> 3

FORM

FORM()

Returns the current setting of NUMERIC FORM.

SAY FORM()
---> SCIENTIFIC
---> ENGINEERING

FORMAT

FORMAT(*number,before decimal,after decimal*)

Formats a *number. Before decimal* is the number of characters before the decimal point, padded with blanks. *After   decimal* is the number of characters after the decimal point, zero filled.

SAY FORMAT(123.45,5,3)
--->   123.450

FUZZ

FUZZ()

Returns the current setting of NUMERIC FUZZ.

SAY FUZZ()
---> 0

INDEX

INDEX(*string,find string*)

Find *find string* within *string*. If not found, return a 0. If found, return the character position of *find string* within *string*.

SAY INDEX('is there a needle in the haystack?','needle')
---> 12

INSERT

INSERT(*string1,string2,position*)

Insert *string1* into *string2* after character *position*.

SAY INSERT('E','ABCDF',4)
---> ABCDEF

JUSTIFY

JUSTIFY(*string,length*)

Create a new string, from *string*, of *length* characters. Justify to both margins by adding blanks between words.

SAY JUSTIFY('Good morning America',40)
---> Good   morning   America

LASTPOS

LASTPOS(*string1,string2*)

Find the last occurence of *string1* in *string2*. Return the character position of the last occurence.

SAY LASTPOS('left','left right left')
---> 12

LEFT

LEFT(*string,length*)

Extract *length* characters from *string* starting at the left.

SAY LEFT('ABCDEF',3)
---> ABC

LENGTH

LENGTH(*string*)

Counts the characters in *string*.

SAY LENGTH('ABCDEF')
---> 6

LINESIZE TSO Only.

LINESIZE()

Returns the current terminal line width, minus 1.

SAY LINESIZE()
---> 79

LISTDSI TSO Only.

DUMMY = LISTDSI(*dataset name*)

Retrieves information about *dataset name*, puts it into variables:

```
SYSDSNAME  <---- the data set name
SYSVOLUME  <---- volume serial number
SYSUNIT    <---- the unit of the above volume
SYSDSORG   <---- PS for sequential
               PO for partitioned
               DA for direct
               VS for VSAM
SYSRECFM   <---- F for fixed           V for variable
               A for ASA printer control  B for blocked
SYSLRECL   <---- Logical record length
SYSBLKSIZE <---- Block size     (VS for VSAM)
SYSKEYLEN  <---- key length
SYSALLOC   <---- space allocation
SYSUSED    <---- space used
SYSPRIMARY <---- primary space allocation
```

```
SYSSECONDS  <---- secondary space allocation
SYSUNITS    <---- space units, CYLINDER, TRACK, BLOCK
SYSEXTENTS  <---- space extents used
SYSCREATE   <---- creation date
SYSREFDATE  <---- date of last reference
SYSEXDATE   <---- expiration date
SYSPASSWORD <---- NONE - no password protection
            READ - read password required
            WRITE - write password required
SYSRACFA    <---- NONE - no RACF protection
            GENERIC - generic profile on this dataset
            DISCRETE - discrete profile on this dataset
SYSUPDATED  <---- YES - has been updated
            NO - not been updated
SYSTRKSCYL  <---- how many tracks per cylinder on the volume
SYSADIRBLK  <---- how many dir blocks allocated
SYSMEMBERS  <---- how many members in the PDS
SYSREASON   <---- reason code for command failure
SYSMSGLVL1  <---- first level error message
SYSMSGLVL2  <---- second level error message
DUMMY       <---- 0 if it worked, 16 if not

        DUMMY = LISTDSI(ABC.DATA)
        /*or*/ LISTDSI("ABC.DATA")
        SAY SYSLRECL
        ---> 80
        /* notice apostrophes on next */
        DUMMY = LISTDSI(" 'SYS1.PROCLIB' ")
        SAY SYSDSORG
        ---> PO
```

MAX

MAX(*number1,number2,....number20*)

Returns the highest of *numbers 1-20*.

```
        SAY MAX(5,4,3,2)
        ---> 5
```

MIN

MIN(*number1,number2,....number20*)

Returns the lowest of *numbers 1-20*.

SAY MIN(5,4,3,2)
---> 2

MSG TSO Only.

MSG()

Returns the current setting of MSG, whether TSO command messages are displayed.

---> ON
---> OFF

SAY MSG()
---> ON

MSG TSO Only.

variable = MSG(on or off)

Returns the current setting of MSG, whether TSO command messages are displayed. A value in the parentheses changes the setting to that value.

---> ON
---> OFF

MESSAGE_VALUE = MSG('OFF') /* value was on. turn it off */
SAY MSG()   /* now it's off */
---> OFF
SAY MSG_VALUE   /* but it was on */
---> ON

OUTTRAP TSO Only.

variable = OUTTRAP('*stem.*')

Turn on capturing of the display output of TSO commands. Each line of output is captured in a different element of the array created from *stem*.

```
stem.0  <---   the number of lines produced
stem.1  <---   the first line
stem.2  <---   the second line, etc.
```

        DUMMY = OUTTRAP('DELCMD.')
        "LISTDS NO.SUCH.DATASET"
        SAY DELCMD.1
        ---> DATASET NO.SUCH.DATASET NOT IN CATALOG

OVERLAY

OVERLAY(*string1*,*string2*,*position*)

Replaces characters in *string2* with characters in *string1* starting in character *position* of *string2*.

        SAY OVERLAY('ABCXEF','D',4)
        ---> ABCDEF

POS

POS(*string1*,*string2*)

Returns the position of *string1* in *string2*. Returns 0 if *string1* is not in *string2*.

        SAY POS('DEF','ABCDEFGHIJKLMNOP')
        ---> 4

PROMPT TSO Only.

PROMPT()

Returns the current setting of PROMPT, whether TSO commands can prompt or not.

---> ON
---> OFF

    SAY PROMPT()
    ---> OFF

PROMPT TSO Only.

variable = PROMPT(on or off)

Returns the current setting of PROMPT, whether TSO commands can prompt or not. A value in the parentheses changes the setting.

---> ON
---> OFF

    PROMPT_VALUE = PROMPT('OFF') /* it was on. turn it off */
    SAY PROMPT()   /* is is off now */
    ---> OFF
    SAY PROMPT_VALUE   /* but it was on */
    ---> ON

QUEUED

QUEUED()

Returns the number of lines in the stack.

    PUSH 'CART'
    SAY QUEUED()
    ---> 1

RANDOM

RANDOM(*min,max*)

Returns a random number between *min* and *max*.

SAY RANDOM(1,100)
---> 55

RANDOM

RANDOM(*min,max,seed*)

Returns a random number between *min* and *max*. Specifying the same *seed* produces the same series each time.

SAY RANDOM(1,100,12345)
---> 55
SAY RANDOM(1,100)
---> 87
SAY RANDOM(1,100,12345)
---> 55
SAY RANDOM(1,100)
---> 87

REVERSE

REVERSE(*string*)

Reverses the characters of the *string*.

SAY REVERSE('GO')
---> OG

RIGHT

RIGHT(*string,length*)

Extract *length* characters from *string* starting at the right.

        SAY RIGHT('ABCDEF',3)
        ---> DEF

SIGN

SIGN(*number*)

Returns the sign of *number*.

    1 <--- if number is positive

    -1 <--- if number is negative

        SAY SIGN(-9)
        ---> -1

SOURCELINE

SOURCELINE(*number*)

Returns original program statement with line number *number*.

        1 /*REXX PROGRAM TO SHOW SOURCELINE*/
        2 SAY SOURCELINE(1)
        ---> /*REXX PROGRAM TO SHOW SOURCELINE*/

SPACE

SPACE(*string,how many blanks*)

Puts *how many blanks* blanks between words in *string*. If *how many blanks* is 0, strips blanks in *string*.

>SAY SPACE('THE FINAL FRONTIER',3)
>---> THE   FINAL   FRONTIER
>
>SAY SPACE('DONT SPACE OUT ON ME',0)
>---> DONTSPACEOUTONME

STRIP

STRIP(*string,option*)

Strips blanks from *string* based on *option*:

>*option*
>   B - remove both leading and trailing blanks (default)
>   T - remove trailing blanks
>   L - remove leading blanks

>SAY STRIP('   MUCH BLANK SPACE ')
>---> MUCH BLANK SPACE

SUBSTR

SUBSTR(*string,start position,length*)

Returns a portion of *string* beginning at *start position* for a length of *length*.

>SAY SUBSTR('PACE',2,3)
>---> ACE

SUBWORD

SUBWORD(*string,starting word,how many words*)

Returns a portion of *string* beginning at *starting word*, containing *how many words* words.

SAY SUBWORD('ET PHONE HOME COLLECT,2,2)
---> PHONE HOME

SYMBOL

SYMBOL(*name*)

Tells if *name* is a variable, literal, or not a legal symbol.

VAR <--- if name is an assigned variable
LIT <--- if name is a literal
BAD <--- if name is not a legal symbol

SAY SYMBOL('*-=:*)
---> BAD
TEAM = 'YANKEES'
SAY SYMBOL(TEAM)
---> VAR
SAY SYMBOL(YANKEES)
---> LIT

SYSDSN TSO Only.

SYSDSN(*dataset name*)

Tells if *dataset name* exists, or what its status is.

OK   <--- dataset name exists as specified.
MEMBER SPECIFIED BUT DATASET
    NOT PARTITIONED   <-- self explanat.
MEMBER NOT FOUND   <-- self explanat.
DATASET NOT FOUND   <-- self explanat.
ERROR PROCESSING REQUESTED DATASET <-- self explanat.
PROTECTED DATASET   <-- self explanat.
VOLUME NOT ON SYSTEM   <-- self explanat.
UNAVAILABLE DATASET   <-- self explanat.
INVALID DATASET NAME   <-- self explanat.
MISSING DATASET NAME   <-- self explanat.


```
IF SYSDSN("JCL.CNTL(JOB001)") = "OK" THEN
DO
    "SUBMIT JCL.CNTL(JOB001)"
END
ELSE DO
    SAY SYSDSN("JCL.CNTL(JOB001)")
END
```

SYSVAR TSO Only.

DUMMY = SYSVAR(*type of info desired*)

Retrieves information about one system variable at a time.

type of info desired:

SYSPREF   ---> the prefix that TSO is putting
in front of dataset names without apostroph.
SYSPROC   ---> the logon procedure used to log on
SYSUID   ---> the userid you logged on with
SYSLTERM   ---> number of lines available on the
terminal screen
SYSWTERM   ---> width of the terminal screen
SYSENV   ---> environment you are executing in
FORE in normal foreground TSO
BACK when executed thru JCL
SYSICMD   ---> the name by which the exec was
executed implicitly
SYSISPF   ---> ACTIVE if dialogue manager is available
NOT ACTIVE if not
SYSNEST   ---> YES if exec executed from another exec/CLIST
NO if executed directly from TSO
SYSPCMD   ---> the most recently executed TSO command
SYSSCMD   ---> the most recently executed TSO subcommand
SYSCPU   ---> how many CPU seconds used so far
SYSHSM   ---> a null, if HSM not available
number indicating release of HSM available
SYSLRACF   ---> a null, if RACF is not installed
number indicating level of RACF available
SYSRACF   ---> AVAILABLE if RACF available
NOT AVAILABLE if RACF not available
NOT INSTALLED if RACF not installed
SYSSRV   ---> how many SRM service units used so far
SYSTSOE   ---> level of TSO/E installed
Syntax error if wrong thing specified

```
       SAY SYSVAR(SYSENV)
       ---> FORE
       SAY SYSVAR(SYSUID)
       ---> TSOU01
```

TRANSLATE

TRANSLATE(*string,output table,input table*)

Translates *string*, converting any occurence of character 1 in *input table* to character 1 of *output table*; character 2 to character 2, etc.

> SAY TRANSLATE('DINERO','NOYEM ','NIREDO')
> ---> MONEY

TRUNC

TRUNC(*number,decimal places*)

Returns the *number* with *"decimal places"* decimal places. Truncates or zero fills as needed.

> SAY TRUNC(1234.5,4)
> ---> 1234.5000

USERID

USERID()

Returns the user id you logged on with.

> SAY USERID()
> ---> TSOU01
> ---> VMUSR1

VALUE

VALUE(*symbol*)

Returns the contents of *symbol* after resolving it as a variable.

```
PROG_NAME = 'COBOL'
COBOL = 'ENGLISH-LIKE'
SAY VALUE('PROG_NAME')
---> COBOL
SAY VALUE(PROG_NAME)
---> ENGLISH-LIKE
```

VERIFY

VERIFY(*string1,string2*)

Are the characters of *string1* made up of characters from *string2*?

if yes, ---> 0
if no, returns the position of first character in *string1*
        that is not in *string2*.

```
SAY VERIFY('SUSAN','ABNTUSV')
---> 0
SAY VERIFY('SUSAN','ABCDEFG')
---> 2
```

WORD

WORD(*string,n*)

Returns the *n*'th word in *string*.

```
SAY WORD('ET PHONE HOME COLLECT,2)
---> PHONE
```

WORDINDEX

WORDINDEX(*string,n*)

Returns the character position of the *n*'th word in *string*.

SAY WORDINDEX('ET PHONE HOME COLLECT',2)
---> 4

WORDLENGTH

WORDLENGTH(*string,n*)

Returns the length of the *n*'th word in *string*.

SAY WORDINDEX('ET PHONE HOME COLLECT',2)
---> 5

WORDPOS

WORDPOS(*phrase,string*)

Searches for *phrase* in *string*. Counts the words in *string* until there is a match. Returns the word count.

SAY WORDPOS('PHONE HOME','ET PHONE HOME COLLECT')

---> 2

WORDS

WORDS(*string*)

Counts the words in *string* Returns the word count.

SAY WORDS('ET PHONE HOME COLLECT')
---> 4

X2C

X2C(*hexstring*)

Converts *hexstring* to character.

SAY X2C('F1F2F3')
---> 123

X2D

X2D(*hexstring*)

Converts *hexstring* to decimal.

SAY X2D('81')
---> 129

Appendix C

INSTRUCTION SUMMARY

This Appendix lists all of REXX's instructions. A brief description of the instruction is given, with a reference to the chapter and paragraph of the text where the instruction is described. The first reference is to the fuller explanation.

ADDRESS   22.5

Directs REXX to pass commands to a specific environment, generally ISPF, the ISPF editor, or TSO.

ARG   16.1   19.2   24.1   24.4   24.7

Short form of PARSE UPPER ARG. In a main program, receives information typed in on the command line next to the name of the program. In a function/subroutine it receives information passed to it on a function invocation, or subroutine call.

CALL   23.1   19.2

Invokes a subroutine, whether internal or external. Turns on or off an error trap that continues executing.

DO   26.1   14.4

Begins a group of instructions that are performed repeatedly, controlled by a variable or a REXX language element.

DROP   See Question 10.3

Undefines a variable. Causes REXX to take the string (which previously was a variable) as a literal, equal to its name, but upper cased.

END   26.1   14.4   21.2

Terminates a group of instructions controlled by a DO. Terminates a SELECT structure.

EXIT   4.1

Ends the REXX program, returns control to the caller, whether the caller is TSO or another program.

EXPOSE   24.2   24.4

Used with the PROCEDURE instruction to allow specific variables to be shared with the main part of the program. Makes those variables global.

IF   14.1

Controls conditional execution of one or more instructions.

INTERPRET   33.1

Makes REXX process a string as a REXX instruction.

ITERATE   24.6

Within a DO END sequence, sends control to the DO, skipping the instructions between it and END.

LEAVE   24.5

Within a DO END sequence, sends control to the statement after the END, thus terminating the loop in an orderly fashion. LEAVE by itself ends the innermost loop. If a loop is controlled by a variable, for example DO I = 1 to 10 you may say LEAVE I to terminate a loop, and any loop nested within it.

NOP   14.3
Null instruction that does nothing. Used in an IF THEN ELSE sequence when no action is desired in an outcome.

NUMERIC   20.3   14.5

NUMERIC DIGITS 14.5   20.3
Sets the precision of arithmetic operations.

NUMERIC FORM   20.3
Sets the way large numbers are shown in exponential notation.

NUMERIC FUZZ   14.5
Controls the number of digits ignored in numeric comparisons.

OTHERWISE   21.2

Introduces the default alternative in the SELECT structure, the path that is taken if no other alternative is true.

PARSE   15.1   15.12   15.13   17.3   27.3

Performs character string manipulation according to various rules that may be specified in the instruction.

PROCEDURE 24.2

Used in an internal function/subroutine to protect the variables of the main part of the program from any possible change, and even from being examined, by the function/subroutine. Makes all variables local.

PULL   27.3   17.1

Short form of PARSE UPPER PULL. Takes a line from the stack, or if it is empty, from the terminal input buffer.

PUSH   27.2

Puts a line consisting of the variables, or literals following it into the stack. Data is put into the stack LIFO.

QUEUE   27.2

Puts a line consisting of the variables, or literals following it into the stack. Data is put into the stack FIFO.

RETURN   19.2   24.1   24.2   24.4

In a function/subroutine sends control back to the instruction after the one which invoked the function/subroutine. Passes back a string of characters to the caller, except in an error trap.

SAY   11.1   20.1

Displays a line on the terminal, consisting of the variables or literals following it.

SELECT   21.2

REXX's implementation of the CASE structure. Allows selection of one of several possible alternatives.

SIGNAL   19.2   19.4   19.5   19.10

Turns on or off an error trap, which can intercept an exceptional condition whenever it occurs after that. May send control unconditionally to a label.

TRACE   18.3   18.4

Controls tracing and interactive debugging.

Appendix D

PROGRAM THAT WILL AUTOMATICALLY CONCATENATE

This Appendix contains a REXX program that will perform a concatenation of your REXX program library to the DDNAME SYSEXEC. It will take into consideration any other library that may be currently allocated to SYSEXEC, and reallocate that library along with your program library.

This program may be executed by an individual after he/she logs on to TSO, or it may be incorporated into an installation's current logon processing.

```
/* REXX program that will automatically concatenate
        your REXX exec library to the DDNAME SYSEXEC.
        The name of the library can be easily changed.
        Type it in carefully */

Add = " 'TSOU01.REXXPRGS.EXEC' " /* LIB to be concaten*/
                                 /* ok to change to any other*/
Thisdd = "SYSEXEC"       /* search for this dd */
                                 /* ok to change to any other */
Found = "NO"
Concat = ""     /* set to null in case DDNAME not alloc*/

Dummy = Outtrap("Sysoutline.","*")/*start capture*/
"LISTALC STATUS"
Dummy = Outtrap("OFF") /*stop capture*/

Do I = 1 while Found = "NO" & I <= Sysoutline.0
   Dsn = Sysoutline.I
   /* Say "looking at " Dsn */
   If Length(Dsn) >= 9
   Then /*length*/
     Do /*length*/
       /* Say "Compare" Substr(Dsn(3,9)*/
       If Substr(Dsn,3,9) = Thisdd
       Then
         Do /*found*/
           Found = "YES"
           I2 = I - 1
           Dsn = Sysoutline.I2
           Concat = "'" || Dsn || "'"
         End /*found*/
       Else I = I + 1
     End /* Length */
   Else I = I + 1 /* Length */
End /* While */
/* Say "At this point, we have picked up " Concat
/* Say "Found status is " Found */
```

Figure D.1. Program that will automatically concatenate. Part 1 of 2.

```
If Found = "YES"
Then
  Do
   Do While (I + 3) <= Sysoutline.0
     Dsn = Sysoutline.I
     /* Say "Comparing " Dsn */
     If Substr(Dsn,1,3) <> "   "
     Then
        Do
          Dsn = Sysoutline.I
          Concat = Concat || " '" || Dsn || "'"
        End
      Else Leave
      I = I + 1
  End /* Do while */
 End /* Found Yes */

 /* Say "At this point, we have picked up " Concat
 /* Ready to allocate */
 Trace C

 "ALLOCATE DDNAME("THISDD") SHR REUSE ",
    "DSNAME("CONCAT ADD")"

  /* LISTALC STATUS */
```

Figure D.2. Program that will automatically concatenate. Part 2 of 2.

Appendix E

USING REXX INSTEAD OF JCL

Topics:

E.1 SOME CONSIDERATIONS

Few installations may be ready at this time to discard their production JCL in favor of REXX execs. I would like, however, to propose a solution to the problem of JCL: run your jobs with REXX execs. There are advantages to this, and disadvantages. First, a production or testing job could be run equally well at the terminal, interactively, or in batch, since the exact same instructions would be processed in either case. A corollary of this is that there would be only one language to learn for processing jobs.

REXX provides clear logic paths, while JCL, at best, provides a very difficult to understand negative type of logic in condition code testing. It is always better to accentuate the positive, and gain control over the flow of processing, than to be subject to an unfriendly type of logic.

Error messages received in batch jobs run with JCL are often cryptic. A REXX program would produce its own error messages, or display those produced by TSO. Normally, your job would not abend or "JCL out", that is, it would not be terminated by the system for attempted violations of system restrictions or invalid JCL syntax. Finally, intelligent recovery from error is possible with REXX's error traps.

On the minus side, I should point out that in most installations it will not be possible to use tape files. At this time it is not possible to use Generation Data Groups since the TSO allocate command does not recognize the name format used by Generation Data Groups. You can expect that a job run with

REXX will require more CPU time than the same job run with JCL. Finally, a knowledge of TSO line mode commands will be required.

At some point in the not too distant future, the advantages will outweigh the disadvantages, and REXX jobs will be the norm. This Appendix will provide the impetus for us to get to that point.

E.2 SAMPLE PRODUCTION JCL

Figure E.1 illustrates a possible set of production JCL that would run a somewhat typical job. This JCL will be converted to a REXX exec.

```
//JOB01 JOB (ACCOUNT),'A.PROGRAMMER',
//       MSGLEVEL=1,CLASS=A
//*
//STEP1     EXEC PGM=PAYPGM
//SYSOUT    DD   SYSOUT=A
//MASTERIN DD    DSN=PAY.B12345.MASTER,
//               DISP=SHR
//TRANSIN   DD   DSN=PAY.B45678.TRANS,
//               DISP=SHR
//MASTOUT   DD   DSN=PAY.B12345.MASTOUT,
//               DISP=(NEW,CATLG),
//               LIKE=(PAY.B12345.MASTER),
//               UNIT=PAYDSK
//*
//STEP2     EXEC PGM=RPTPGM
//REPORT    DD   SYSOUT=A,DEST=PRT3800
//SYSOUT    DD   SYSOUT=A
//REPRTIN   DD   DSN=PAY.B12345.MASTOUT,
//               DISP=SHR
```

Figure E.1. Typical production JCL.

E.3 REXX EXEC THAT REPLACES SAMPLE JCL

Figures E.2 and E.3 illustrate a possible implementation of a REXX exec that would do the same thing as the JCL in Figure E.1. A few things are worth pointing out. First, it asks the system if it is executing in foreground, that is interactively under TSO. If so, it asks the user if it should continue. If not, it stops. An error trap is set up, so that any command failure can be intercepted and the erroneous statement displayed. The allocations are done next. If any of these should fail, control will go to the error trap. Then the first program is executed with the statement "PAYPGM". In some installations, the program will have to be executed with a TSO CALL command. After the program is executed, the allocations are freed, and the allocations for the next program are done. Finally the message is displayed that the job completed successfully.

```
/* REXX payjob */
TRACE ALL
If Sysvar("SYSENV") = "FORE"
Then
   Do
     Say "This is Payjob. should execution continue? Y/N"
     Pull Reply
     If Reply = "Y" | Reply = "YES" then Nop
   End
Else Exit
Signal on Error
"ALLOC SYSOUT(A) DDN(SYSOUT)"
"ALLOC DSN('PAY.B12345.MASTER') SHR DDN(MASTERIN)"
"ALLOC DSN('PAY.B45678.TRANS') SHR DDN(TRANSIN)"
If Sysdsn("'PAY.B12345.MASTOUT'") = "OK"
Then
   Do
     "ALLOC DSN('PAY.B12345.MASTOUT') SHR DDN(MASTOUT)"
   End
Else
   Do
     "ALLOC DSN('PAY.B12345.MASTOUT') SHR DDN(MASTOUT)",
         "LIKE('PAY.B12345.MASTER')"
   End
   "PAYPGM" /* execute program */
/* may need to execute this way:
     "CALL PROGLIB(PAYPGM)"*/
"FREE DDN(SYSOUT MASTERIN TRANSIN MASTOUT)"
"ALLOC DDN(REPRTIN) DSN('PAY.B12345.MASTOUT') SHR"
"ALLOC SYSOUT(A) DEST(PRT3800) DDN(REPORT)"
"ALLOC SYSOUT(A) DDN(SYSOUT)"
"RPTPGM"
/* may need to execute this way:
     "CALL PROGLIB(RPTPGM)"*/
"FREE DDN(REPRTIN SYSOUT REPORT)"
Say "job completed successfully"
Exit
```

Figure E.2. REXX exec executing the job in sample JCL. Part 1 of 2.

```
Error:
Say "error occured in payjob "
Say "Source statment " Sourceline(sigl)
Say "Error code     " Rc
Say "Error:         " Errortext(RC)
Exit
```

Figure E.3. REXX exec executing the job in sample JCL. Part 2 of 2.

E.4 JCL NEEDED TO RUN THE REXX EXEC

A small amount of JCL is still needed, in order to run the REXX exec (see Figure E.4). This JCL will be the same for virtually all jobs that an installation runs, thus eliminating the need for extensive knowledge of JCL. Please note that the PARM statement contains the name of the REXX exec PAYJOB. Putting the name of an exec there causes the exec to be executed automatically. A percent sign was used, to speed up execution. The name of the REXX program library must be present on a SYSEXEC DD statement.

```
//JOB01 JOB (ACCOUNT),'A. PROGRAMMER',
//       MSGLEVEL=1,CLASS=A
//TSO   EXEC PGM=IKJEFT01,
//       DYNAMBR=20,
//       PARM='%PAYJOB'
//SYSTSPRT DD SYSOUT=A
//SYSTSIN  DD DUMMY
//SYSEXEC  DD DSN=SYSTEM.REXXEXCS.EXEC,DISP=SHR
```

Figure E.4. JCL to run the REXX exec.

INDEX